400 Steals Beyond Belief

The essential almanac to a freer world

By Eric W. Gershman

Financial Answers Network, Inc.
129 South Street
Boston, MA 02111

About the author

Eric W. Gershman is one of the industry's top experts on financial communications. He is president of Published Image, Inc., a Boston-based newsletter company whose 40 different publications reach more than 12 million investors a year.

Profiled by *The Wall Street Journal* and New England Cable News for his innovative approach to saving money through savvy management Mr. Gershman shares his most imaginative strategies in this well-researched and highly entertaining book.

Copies of this book can be obtained from your local bookstore or the publisher:

Financial Answers Network, Inc.
129 South Street
Boston, MA 02111

Or call 1-800-411-6789

FIRST EDITION 1996

Designed by Jon Delongchamp and edited by Quality Works.
Illustrated by Nicola Valentino.

ISBN 0-9648996-0-4

Contents

Author's Note

I am a successful business person who can afford almost anything I want. Yet, one way I got there was taking advantage of every steal, and every legal opportunity I could. I'm not talking about coupons or chintzy calendars emblazoned with company names. I only go for high quality. It's been years since I embarked on this journey to obtain what's coming to me. Now I invite you to take a peek. So get into the mindset, hold onto your wallet, suspend skepticism and grab the goods. Let me know about treasures you've unearthed, so I can include them in the next volume. Oh, and a special thank you to the new Gran-C, Grand-Bob, my darling Robin and all the airlines that started these thoughts!

Enjoy,

Eric
egershman@pubimage.com

Chapter One

TRAVEL TROVE

Here's how to get everything from free ski trips in Colorado to free movie tickets for the latest releases.

1 SKI FREE IN COLORADO.

Don't dismiss all travel deals as scams. Granted, postcards from Florida offering free vacations and cruises for $199 are thinly disguised tricks to get your credit card number. But legitimate resorts do offer some incredible freebies. For example, since 1990, Crested Butte, Colo. (800-SKI-FREE), has sponsored Ski Free days between Thanksgiving and Christmas. Because Crested Butte requires a five-hour drive from Denver, the ski resort found its popularity lagging the more accessible mountains. To encourage skiers to try the resort, which has some of the West's best black diamond slopes, the resort waives the lift-ticket charge ($42 a day) for those days. Skiers who are brand new to the sport also get free "never ever" ski lessons ($46 value) for those 7 or older. This year the deal runs Nov. 17-Dec. 16 and from April 8-21 in 1996. Another bonus: When you ride the Mountain Express coming from the airport, you'll be given a discount booklet for area restaurants and ski shops.

Kids are king at the resort, too. Children 12 and under pay their age to ski with one adult paying full price. No blackout periods, no limit on the number of children and no minimum on the days or lodging are required.

2 FREE BROADWAY SHOWS.

To get into top-flight theatrical events, call the manager of your local venue and volunteer your services as an usher or ticket seller. Your return for spending an hour guiding people to their seats? After you've done your duty, you are free to watch the show from your own seat. Not a bad take when you consider the tickets for touring Broadway shows usually go for at least $50 apiece. (This technique won't work in the Big Apple where all ushering assignments are paid positions.)

3 BROADWAY AT HALF PRICE.

Tickets to the best shows on Broadway are nearing the $100 mark, so unless you're independently wealthy, you should check into tickets for less than the masses are paying. Here are two sources:

The Hit Show Club (630 Ninth Ave., New York, N.Y. 10036; 212-581-4211) publishes coupons that get you a discount at the box office. Get a list of currently discounted shows by sending a SASE a month before you plan to attend.

TKTS booths are the other option. One is in Times Square (47th and Broadway) and another, lesser known location is at 2 World Trade Center. Yet another is in downtown Brooklyn at the intersection of Court and Montague streets. On the day of the performance, you wait in line and get tickets at half price. Of course, this strategy is foolhardy if you're hoping for a hot show on Broadway. However, for the oldies but goodies, you'll probably come away feeling smug.

4 THE PERFORMING ARTS FOR LESS.

Many cities have special groups formed to support performances, but give members deep discounts on tickets. For example, in New York, contact the The Theater Development Fund (1501 Broadway, Suite 2110, New York, N.Y. 10036; information line 212-221-0013 or main office 212-221-0885). Send a SASE, for a group ($50) or individual ($14) application. If you are accepted, you'll receive offers for deep discounts on many events and shows.

5 TRAVEL DEALS FOR GENERATION X AND YOUNGER.

If you are under 26 and older than 12 or a full-time teacher, you are eligible for membership in the Council on International Educational Exchange (205 E. 42nd St., New York, N.Y. 10017; 212-661-1414), which gives you a special card good for discounts on everything from airfare to accommodations. It's an especially good deal if you're traveling to Europe. This non-profit organization also puts out a free magazine called Travel!. Request a free copy when you write.

A division of CIEE, Council Travel often has good deals on airfares, railroad passes, accommodations and car rentals. It has offices in many major cities around the country including: Atlanta 404-377-9997, Austin 512-472-4931, Boulder 303-447-8101, Boston 617-266-1926, Chicago 312-951-0585, Los Angeles 818-905-5777, Miami 305-670-9261, Minneapolis 612-379-2323, New York 212-661-1450, San Francisco 415-421-3473, Seattle 206-632-2448 and Washington, D.C. 202-337-6464.

6 TRY HOSTELLING FOR YOUNG AND OLD.

Becoming a member of Hostelling International (733 15th St. N.W., Suite 840, Washington, D.C. 20013-7613; 202-783-6161; membership is $25 if you're between 18 and 54; $15 otherwise) gives you access to more than 5,000 hostels in 70 countries (price range $5-22 a night; cheaper than camping fees in many instances). For guaranteed reservations, call 800-444-6111.

A one-year family membership to the American Youth Hostel Organization (202-783-4943) costs $35 and gets you discounts on stays, travel books and gear.

7 TAKE A CROSS-COUNTRY DRIVE FOR THE COST OF GAS ONLY.

If you're the adventurous sort, you can get the free use of a car (first tank of gas included) to get to one of 75 destination cities. You must be 21 years old and put down a $250-400 security deposit refunded when you deliver the car. A friend can accompany you on your journey. For more details, contact Auto Driveaway Co., 310 South Michigan Ave., Chicago, Ill. 60604 or 800-346-2277.

8 GETTING TICKETS FOR HARD-TO-SEE EVENTS.

Want to go to the Superbowl, the Olympics, the Masters or some other blockbuster event for which tickets are in short supply? Graciously volunteer to act as a host for visiting dignitaries. For example, for the 1996 Summer Olympic Games in Atlanta more than 40,000 volunteers will be tapped and get tickets to an event or two in exchange for their good turn. (Interested Georgia residents should call Atlanta Committee for the Olympic Games at 404-224-1996.) For cities trying to put on a good face, good will is important and anyone who helps garner it from tourists will be rewarded.

9 GET A PERSONALIZED TOUR OF THE WHITE HOUSE — FREE.

If you're planning a trip to Washington, D.C., call your local U.S. representative for free congressional perks like passes to the House and Senate galleries and a VIP tour of the White House, sparing you the long wait the teeming masses endure. (The main number is 202-225-3121.) If you have children, mention their ages and you'll likely get free tickets to attractions they would enjoy, too.

10 TRAVEL FOR FREE.

Okay, so Condé Nast Traveler won't even consider using your beautifully written account of frolicking in Morocco if you accepted a free ride to get there. But who cares? Travel is one of the biggest industries worldwide, and demand for writing about places near and far is insatiable. If you have a flair for writing, that talent could get you a free vacation. The trick is getting that first assignment. Contact your local newspaper, travel newsletters or other publications that carry travel stories and pitch your latest vacation. If you have great photos to accompany your words, all the better.

Once you have one article published—called a clip in free-lance writer jargon—you may be able to parlay that into real assignments. When you want to travel to a certain city, contact all the publications you can think of and ask if they'd take a piece on that destination. Even if the editor says, "Okay, but only on spec," you're off and running. "On spec" means maybe your article will be published and maybe not, depending on whether the editor likes the finished product. But you've still got a legitimate assignment. Next, call the Visitors and Convention Bureau, and tell them you'd like to visit, because you write for such-and-such publication. Sometimes you'll be referred to a public relations outfit handling the town's press.

At the very least, you'll be referred to hotels and restaurants where you can announce that you are a travel writer and hope for royal treatment. If the publication rates well with the public relations folks and you have an assignment letter, you'll rate red carpet treatment with free passes to all the main attractions and free food. You can also target a particular resort. If the resort doesn't offer free lodging, ask for the writer's rate, which is often ridiculously low. Free airfare can be much more difficult to obtain, but isn't impossible. If you are writing for the airline's magazine or if your public relations representative can swing it, you'll fly free, too. Contacting the airline's public relations department usually doesn't work. However, foreign airlines are sometimes eager to host travel writers and are much less in demand than domestics.

Another good source for you, once you have some published articles, is Working Writer (130 W. 80th St., Suite 2F, New York, N.Y. 10024; 212-874-3367; monthly annual subscription $70).

Check with your local community college or adult learning center for classes on travel writing. A handy book with 20,000 listings of who's who in the travel industry is Fairchild's Travel Industry Personnel Directory ($30), which you can order by calling 800-247-6622.

11 Cruises for Free.

Use that handy-dandy Fairchild directory (page 6) to check out cruise lines. Although the Internal Revenue Service has cracked down on writing off cruises for educational purposes, you may still be able to do even better. You and your spouse (or companion) can score a terrific cruise if you have a marketable talent like teaching creative writing or leading an estate planning seminar that the cruise director would like to highlight. With competition so stiff for passengers, cruise ships are looking for anything that will give them a leg up. Some of the major cruise lines are: Carnival Cruise Lines (800-327-2058); Cunard Line (800-5-CUNARD) and Royal Cruise Line (800-227-4534). Call the entertainment office of the cruise line of your choice, and sell yourself. Then once you've taught a class or given your talk or performance, you're free to lounge about on the deck with the rest of the paying tourists—except your passage won't cost you a dime.

Similarly, if you are an entertainer, an outfit like Club Med (800-CLUBMED) may give you a week's vacation in return for crooning for the masses a night or two during your stay. We were in Club Med Huatulco when an a capella quintet from Princeton did exactly that.

12 Liven Up Your Vacation With Freebies.

When you've got your heart set on a certain spot, call 800-555-1212 and see if there is a toll-free number for the Visitors and Convention Bureau. Then call and ask for a packet of tourist information. You'll get free maps and other goodies. Ask if there are any special deals coming up. Some tourist areas are so eager for business that local merchants all pitch in to sweeten the pot for you. For example, even though St. Croix, part of the U.S. Virgin Islands in the Caribbean, has long since recovered from Hurricane Hugo, tourism has still been down. So for the past few years, local hotels have offered a free rental car to anyone staying five days or more. In Orlando, Fla., tourists who know to ask are sent a Magicard (800-643-9492), or this special card can be picked up at visitors' centers. That card gives you 20-50% off at hundreds of attractions in Orlando.

Chattanooga (800-322-3344), home of the popular freshwater Tennessee Aquarium, and Nashville, known as Music City U.S.A. (615-259-4730), both in Tennessee, each give visitors savvy enough to ask booklets packed with coupons for everything from restaurants to hotels to attractions. You can sometimes find special discount booklets at welcome centers on the state borderline. Ask the staff on duty, because they aren't always displayed.

13 TEST SPORTING GOODS FOR FREE.

The gear required for outdoor sports like kayaking, rock climbing, fishing and skiing can easily set you back several hundred dollars. Familiarize yourself with the necessary equipment by visiting local sporting goods stores. Some stores like Recreational Equipment, Inc. (800-426-4840) even have areas where you can test the equipment for free and have experts teach free clinics on water and snow sports. You can also call its toll-free hotline with questions about gear. Compare prices between the most reputable discount catalogers—Bass Pro Shops (800-227-7776 or 417-887-1915), Sierra Trading Post (307-775-8000) or Campmor (800-230-2151)—with a local sporting goods store that offers discounts. Carry the catalog into your local store and see if it will match the discounted price.

14 CAMP FOR FREE.

After camping for four years full-time, Mary Helen and Shuford Smith have compiled two terrific books: Camp the U.S. for $5 or Less: Western States and Camp the U.S. for $5 or Less: Eastern States (each $13.95 at your bookstore or order from Globe Pequot Press at 800-243-0495; in Connecticut 800-962-0973. The PIB numbers for ordering are 1-56-440-173-1 and 1-56-440-287-8 respectively). Although camping can be expensive, the Smiths have unearthed thousands of sites that are inexpensive or even free. Often, campers are asked only to perform some chore in exchange for occupying a camp site.

15 VACATION ABROAD—AND STAY FOR (ALMOST) FREE.

If your house is in a desirable area and has some nice amenities, you may be able to write your own ticket by swapping your abode for a vacation abroad. Several outfits serve as clearinghouses for such swaps. You'll have to pay a fee (usually around $50) to be listed in a catalog. Just make sure you lay out the ground rules before the trading family arrives. If you find a match who wants what you have, you'll have a vacation spot with all the conveniences of home, yet your only real expenses will be for transportation and food—meaning whopping savings of $3,000 or more on hotel rooms, $500-1,000 on car rentals and $500-1,000 by cooking meals at the house. Call the Invented City (800-788-2489); Vacation Exchange Club (800-638-3841); Intervac International Home Exchange (415-435-3497 or fax 415-435-7440, which has more than 9,000 homes in more than 30 countries) or Loan-A-Home (914-664-7640), which specializes in long-term exchanges.

16 DISCOUNT TRAVEL CLUBS.

You can travel at less than half the going rate, if you join a travel club. Typically, you will either get a discount book or a card that looks like a credit card and is shown to participating merchants. Get the directory and scan the hotels and resorts you plan to visit. Call the hotel reservation desk directly and ask for rates and availability. Then identify yourself as a club member and ask what the discounted rate will be. Ask about special promotions, too. Sometimes those can be even better than your membership. Once the reservation is made, guarantee it with a credit card and obtain a confirmation number. Don't forget to show your card or coupon upon arrival.

Some of the best clubs:

Entertainment Publications (800-477-3234) sells packed coupon books for 130 cities in the U.S., Canada and the Caribbean for an average of $38 that knock off 50% on hotels and 20% on restaurants and other discounts at stores, local attractions, airlines, car rentals, and sporting events. If you buy the local book, you are then entitled to buy five other books at a $28 each through the Extradition Program.

Encore (800-638-8976; $49).

Great American Traveler (800-548-2812; $49.95) gives 50% off at 2,400 hotels as well as discounts with Alamo.

World Hotel Express (800-634-6526; $49.95).

Quest International Corporation (800-560-4100 or 800-638-9819; $99 for individual member/$30 each per association member) gives you 50% off at 2,100 hotels, as well as discounts on cruises, condominiums and airlines. You also get 25% off at 350 restaurants nationwide.

17 GET THE FREEBIES YOU DESERVE.

Don't go away mad. Let someone know what went awry—whether it's your luggage or your room-service breakfast. Airlines, hotels and some rental car companies are especially sensitive to customer complaints. Tell a customer service representative specifically what would satisfy you. If you don't immediately get help from customer service, ask for the president or regional manager's address and follow up with a written complaint. Keep a letter factual, short and unemotional. For the five minutes it takes to write a letter, you'll probably get a certificate worth $100 or so for your next go-round with the company.

For example, one passenger's American Eagle flight from South Georgia was canceled with no notice and no explanation, necessitating a two-hour drive north to Atlanta to catch a connecting flight on another airline that had agreed to honor the ticket back to New York. Upon arriving at the airport in Atlanta, the agent for another airline who had agreed to honor the ticket noticed that the ticket was written as though the trip was originating from New York instead of Atlanta. That boggle by the gate agent in South Georgia almost cost the traveler a seat on that return flight as well. A letter to the airline whose agent made the original mistake brought an apology and a $100 travel certificate.

18 OFF-SEASON SKIING.

Get 40% off your skiing by waiting until the weather begins to warm up toward the end of March. Spring skiing at some resorts lasts until early June. Resorts often kick-in ski passes and other deep discounts. Here are some popular resorts worth checking with:
Vermont's Killington 800-372-2007
Sunday River at Bethel, Maine 800-543-2754
Club Tremblant in Canada 800-363-2413
Whistler/Blackcomb in British Columbia 800-944-7853
Snowbird in Utah 800-453-3000
Crested Butte in Colorado 800-SKI-FREE
Vail/Beaver Creek 800-525-2257.

19 TRAVELING FREE WITH CHILDREN.

If you are traveling with kids, look for national chains that give free lodging and food for the tykes. Recognizing families as a boon for business, hoteliers are no longer disdainful of youngsters. Hyatt Hotels (800-233-1234), Howard Johnson (800-654-2000), Hilton Hotels (800-HILTONS), Best Western (800-528-1234), Choice Hotels (800-424-6423), Marriott

(800-321-CLUB) and Holiday Inn (800-HOLIDAY) are just a few of the chains that offer free stays, free meals and other goodies for kids. Best Western's Young Travelers Club (kids 16 and under), for example, rewards frequent stays with bonus points redeemable for such perks as certificates of deposit and U.S. savings bonds. They also get an Official Adventure Card, an Adventure Pack and Journal and a bimonthly newsletter.

Even the upscale Ritz-Carlton Hotel Company (800-241-3333), for instance, has a suite for kids. It is packed with videos, games, toys and a fridge stocked with age-appropriate goodies, at no extra charge. Compare the chains' programs by calling their toll-free numbers.

Club Med (800-CLUBMED) has gotten in on the family vacation action, too, recognizing that its swinging singles market has shifted to aging baby-boomers with tots in tow. If you have older children, Club Med's Family Escape packages offer the best deal, shaving $500-700 a person off the cost. If your children are under 5, ask about its "Kids Free" weeks, available at six resorts.

20 RENTAL CAR WARS.

When making any transaction, ask if the company has a booklet with tips on getting more bang for your buck. Alamo Rent-A-Car teamed up with the Association of Consumer Agency Administrators to produce A Consumer's Guide to Renting a Car, a handy booklet surprisingly free of self-promotion. (Send a 32-cent stamped, self-addressed envelope to McCool Communications, P.O. Box 13005, Atlanta, Ga. 30324 with your request or call 404-814-1936.)

Because several rental car companies are owned by big car manufacturers, fewer new cars are being sold to rental companies. What that means to you is that you are more likely to get stuck with a car that has high mileage, and is therefore more prone to breakdowns. When you reserve the car, request that you be given the car on the lot with the least amount of miles on it. Also, ask that a cellular phone be pitched in for free. Several companies are now providing them because of the wave of violence against tourists in rental cars. If you have a child, rental companies are also required to give you a car-seat, free of charge.

Don't be bamboozled into buying more car rental insurance than you need. Agents typically get a commission on sales of the Collision Damage Waiver, which can double the cost of your rental. You are likely already covered on your auto insurance policy. However, check with your agent before you rent. At present, Diner's Club is the only charge card that offers primary insurance on rental cars. Several of the other card issuers have quietly lowered the amount they will pay on accidents and theft for rental cars or have dropped the service completely. Call the toll-free number on the back of your credit card to find out exactly what coverage you get before putting the charge on that card. Here are the majors and their toll-free numbers: Alamo Rent-A-Car (800-327-0400); Auto Europe (800-223-5555); Avis (800-331-1212); Budget (800-527-0700); Eurodollar Rent A Car Ltd. (800-800-6000); Hertz (800-654-3131); Thrifty (800-FORCARS) and Value (800-GO VALUE).

To get the best deals on rental cars overseas, prepay before you leave the U.S. or you may find yourself at the mercy of rental agencies who gouge the prices. Remember that automatic transmission and air conditioning are not standard and requesting either can significantly jack up the price. You may also want to rent a compact car because roads in foreign countries are often significantly narrower and a smaller car will be easier to manuever.

21 TRAVEL FREE FOR BEING AN EXPERT.

If you are an expert in economics, international affairs, litera-
ture, the arts, U.S. political or social policies, sports, science or
technology, your knowledge could be your free ticket to foreign
countries. For a free brochure explaining lecture opportunities
with the United States Information Agency (USIA), write
American Experts Overseas Lecture Tour, Office of Program
Coordination and Development, USIA, 301 Fourth St. S.W.,
Room 550, Washington, D.C. 20547 or call 202-619-4764.

22 GETTING DISCOUNTS ON HOTEL ROOMS.

If you want to stay at a good hotel without going into sticker
shock, there is a way. First, look at ratings in the AAA
Tourbook (available to American Automobile Association
members 407-444-8000), Mobil Travel Guide (Prentice Hall
Travel $13.95 or Prodigy's on-line service) or make a free call
to your travel agent and ask for hotels with a Mobil two-star
rating or AAA three-star rating and above, at your destination
city. Courtyard by Marriott, Fairfield Inn by Marriott, La
Quinta, the Ritz-Carlton and Four Seasons all are consistently
good as well.

Call the free reservation numbers and ask for the weekend
rate, or for a weekday stay, ask what deals are available. Never
take the first quote (called the rack rate). Press for a cheaper
rate. Nine times out of 10, you'll get it. Once you've gotten a
quote, call the hotel directly. Often, individual hotels are running specials that central reservations don't know about. Or
they may be included in the hotel directory of a travel club, in
which case you must call and give your membership number.
These directories usually get you 50% or more off the rack rate.
You may also be able to get a discount by charging the room on
a certain credit card. Be sure to ask about special promotions
for certain charge cards.

Another new way to get deep discounts on great rooms is through discount reservation services that specialize in big cities across the country. Operating somewhat like airline consolidators, these services offer rooms at huge savings (up to 65%) when hoteliers are anticipating lots of vacancies. Here are several services and the cities in which they specialize:

Accommodations Express, 800-444-7666: Atlantic City, Chicago, Las Vegas, Miami, New York, Orlando, Philadelphia and Washington, D.C.

Capitol Reservations, 800-847-4832: Washington, D.C.

California Reservations, 800-576-0003: California, Seattle and Portland, Ore.

Central Reservations Service, 800-950-0232: Los Angeles, Miami, New York, Orlando, San Francisco.

City Wide Reservations, 800-733-6644: Las Vegas and Laughlin, Nevada.

Express Reservations, 800-356-1123: New York and Los Angeles.

Golden Gate Reservations, 800-576-0003: San Francisco and most major cities in California, Portland and Seattle.

Hot Rooms, 800-468-3500: Chicago.

Hotels Plus, 800-235-0909: Hotels in continental Europe and bed-and-breakfasts in Ireland, Scotland, the United Kingdom and Wales.

Hotel Reservations Network, 800-964-6835: Atlanta, Baltimore, Boston, Chicago, Dallas, Honolulu, Maui, London, Los Angeles, Miami, New Orleans, New York, Orlando, Paris, Philadelphia, San Diego, San Francisco, Seattle, Washington.

Meegan Hotel Reservations Services, 800-332-3026: Boston.

San Francisco Reservations, 800-677-1550: San Francisco.

The Room Exchange, 800-846-7000: Major U.S. cities.

Quickbook, 800-789-9887: in 21 cities including Atlanta, Baltimore, Boston, Chicago, Cincinnati, Dallas, Denver, Houston, Los Angeles, Maui, Miami, Minneapolis, Montreal,

Nashville, New Orleans, New York, Philadelphia, Portland, Ore., San Diego, San Francisco, Seattle.

These services are absolutely free. But you have to give your credit card number for a deposit at the time of booking, and show your card or coupon when you check in.

23 EAT FREE IN YOUR FAVORITE RESTAURANT.

If you've always wanted to be a restaurant critic, now is your chance. Restaurant and Hotel Services reimburses shoppers for restaurant meals and bar tabs for two. The average check is $20-120 at restaurants ranging from chains like T.G.I. Friday's to pricey Morton's of Chicago. To become a shopper, call Restaurant and Hotel Services (703-591-6729) and leave your name and address. You'll be sent a two-page application and be asked to write about a recent restaurant experience, giving details like how long it took to get seated, the restaurant's cleanliness and how long it took between courses. Shoppers who do a good job are promoted to making secret visits to hotels. Health clubs also sometimes employ secret shoppers. After each experience you must turn in a detailed report in a timely manner.

Shop and Check (800-669-6526) operates a similar service for retail stores, gas stations, fast-food restaurants, eyeglass stores and restaurants. For an application, write Shop and Check, P.O. Box 28175, Atlanta, Ga. 30358-0175.

You can also exert your opinion with Zagat's Guides (800-333-3421). Those who participate in Zagat's annual restaurant surveys are rewarded with a free guide for their city (value $9.95-16.95). To get a survey, send a SASE and a note requesting a survey for a restaurant, hotel and shop to: Zagat Survey, 4 Columbus Circle, New York, N.Y. 10019.

24 GET 25% OFF YOUR RESTAURANT TAB.

The IGT Charge Card (800-444-8872) gives you 25% off your tab, excluding tax and tip. The annual fee is $48, but you may be able to negotiate to have the first year free. Indeed, that is a perk for Chase Manhattan Visa cardholders, who can then renew for $25. Get IGT's free brochure of participating restaurants to see if it makes it a good deal for you.

Premiere Dining (800-346-3241) gives you 2-for-1 dining at more than 9,000 restaurants nationwide. Annual dues are $49 or you can try it for three months for $1.99. You also get discount coupons for movies and fast-food.

25 TINY AIRFARES TO EXOTIC PLACES.

If traveling alone and at the drop of a hat appeals to you, you'd make a perfect courier. You have to make do with a single carry-on but you can get tickets to exotic locations like Rio de Janeiro and Hong Kong for as little as $50 roundtrip, if you're flexible. Your two suitcases will be used to transport freight. Trips are typically for one week, sometimes two. On rare occasions, you might be able to stay as long as 90 days. International flights departing from JFK International in New York, Newark in New Jersey and Miami International are available from Now Voyager (212-431-1616) or Courier Travel Service (516-763-6898 or fax 516-374-2261). The latter specializes in Western Europe, South America, Hong Kong and Tel Aviv, and it will send you a free information pack on being a courier. If the idea of being a courier appeals to you, you might want to order a copy of The Courier Air Travel Handbook (Thunderbird Press, 5501 North Seventh Ave., Suite 116, Phoenix, Ariz. 85031; 800-359-1616; $12.95).

26 FREE TICKETS TO TELEVISION TAPINGS.

You don't have to spend big bucks to attend television tapings. In fact, most shows will allow you to attend for free. In most cases, you have to send in your request at least six weeks prior to your visit. At the end of your favorite show that's taped live, you'll find instructions on where to write for tickets. Or send a SASE with your ticket request to:

ABC Tickets, 4151 Prospect Ave., Los Angeles, Calif. 90027
CBS Tickets, 7800 Beverly Blvd., Los Angeles, Calif. 90036
NBC Tickets, 3000 West Alameda Blvd., Burbank, Calif. 91523.

Tickets to two popular game shows can be tapped, too:
Wheel of Fortune (213-852-2458).
Jeopardy!, 10202 W. Washington Blvd., Culver City, Calif. 90232.

If you are a country music fan, contact Gaylord Entertainment (615-883-7000), which tapes several country music shows in Nashville. For free tickets to the Nashville's Wildhorse Saloon Dance, shown on TNN and a country version of American Bandstand, write: P.O. Box 148400, Nashville, Tenn. 37214 and send a SASE, or call 615-885-1593.

27 FREE U.S. TOURIST ATTRACTIONS.

For a complete state-by-state listing of free U.S. attractions, send $5.95 + $1.50 shipping and handling for The National Directory of Free Tourist Attractions, Pilot Books, 103 Cooper St., Babylon, N.Y. 11702; 516-422-2225.

28 TAKING WASHINGTON, D.C. FOR FREE.

One of the best places in the world to visit if you're short of cash but long on curiosity is our nation's capital, which has almost 50 free places of interest. For a free booklet listing this treasure trove of free sites, contact: D.C. Convention and

Visitors Association, 1212 New York Ave. N.W., Suite 200, Washington, D.C. 20005; 202-724-4091. The Gold Mine Directory lists almost 2,000 Washington businesses that give special discounts to seniors and students.

29 FREE INSIDE STUFF FROM TRAVEL PROS.

If you are on the road a lot, there are several handy publications that will help you get big discounts and travel smart. Each of these will send you a free sample copy, of course. Here are some of the best:

Best Fares ($58 a year, 800-635-3033) is a monthly magazine detailing the best airfare deals and dozens of other discounts from travel vendors.

Flyer's Edge ($18.95 a year, 800-248-1826) is a quarterly booklet listing changes to the frequently changing, frequent-traveler programs.

Frequent Flyer ($24 a year; 12 issues; 800-323-3537) is a monthly, glossy news magazine with lots of good consumer news.

InsideFlyer ($33 a year; 12 issues; 800-333-5937) lasers in on frequent flyer news and tips. It's produced by the expert in the field, Randy Petersen.

The Ticket ($34 a year; monthly; 404-266-1140), written by Chris McGinnis of the Travel Skills Group, this information-packed newsletter gives terrific business tips, especially for Atlanta-based travelers.

30 BED AND BREAKFAST ON A BUDGET.

If you enjoy the coziness of staying in a private home or small inn, make a free call to get some guidance for your ramblings: Bed and Breakfast International 800-872-4500. It specializes in free reservations in California and will refer you to B&B reservation services nationwide and in Europe (most make reservations free; some charge a nominal fee) that will match your dreams to the perfect spot.

31 ZAP HAIR-RAISING HOTEL TELEPHONE BILLS.

Before you start burning up the wires wheeling and dealing, ask the front desk about the surcharges on phone calls that may apply even if you use a calling card. (Hilton and Stouffer's dropped the extra charges due to customer complaints.) If there is a surcharge (usually 50 cents to $1 per call), only pay once by pressing the # key for two seconds at the end of your call and then dialing the next number. Or use the pay phone in the lobby area. In nicer hotels, you'll find somewhat comfy private booths from which to conduct your business.

32 SAVE BIG BUCKS ON AIRFARE THROUGH COUPON BROKERS.

Coupon brokers match travelers who want to sell a discounted or frequent flyer certificate to those who want to buy them. They are matchmakers. The rub is that purchasing one of these tickets is against airline rules—not the law. Airlines are within their rights to pull your ticket if you are discovered using a brokered ticket. However, that rarely happens. One of the most reputable coupon brokers is International Air Coupon Exchange (2755 South Locust St., Suite 119, Denver, Colo. 80222; 800-558-0053 or fax 303-753-0728), which guarantees its customers' tickets. The real savings with a broker come if you want to fly first or business class. Brokers can no longer be very competitive with supersaver fares. A spokesman gave this example: "A flight from the East Coast to Australia would cost $7,000-8,000 first class during the peak season, while our ticket year-round would be about $2,800 roundtrip. We can usually save consumers 50-70% off when they're traveling business or first class." The coupons are also valid for a year, and you can make any date changes with no penalties whatsoever.

33 USE A TRAVEL AGENT FOR FREE.

Few people have enough information to be doing their own travel arrangements. Using a travel agent is free for the consumer. They will work hard to get you the best fares and rates and deliver tickets right to your office or home. Contact the American Society of Travel Agents (703-739-2782).

34 GET 50% OFF AIRLINE TICKETS THROUGH CONSOLIDATORS.

Consolidators buy up seats on undersold routes and pass along the wholesale prices to consumers. You can get especially good deals—as much as 50% off—to Europe. Here are some popular companies:

Access International 800-333-7280 (Western and Eastern Europe and the Middle East);

Council Charter 800-890-8222 (Caribbean, Central America, Europe and Martinique);

Jetway 800-421-8771 (Asia, China, Europe, South Pacific);

Picasso Travel 800-525-3632;

Queue Travel Inc., 1530 West Lewis St., San Diego, Calif. 92103, 800-356-4871 (more than 30,000 special airfare deals from 28 major airlines servicing the U.S., Europe, Asia, Latin America, the South Pacific, Russia, Eastern Europe and Africa).

35 BEAT EXPENSIVE AIRLINE PRICES WITH HIDDEN CITY FARES.

Airlines often run specials to certain destinations and even if they are farther in distance than you want to go, check to see if the "hidden city" fare game will net you big savings. Here's how it works: Book a one-way flight to a less expensive city with a layover at your true destination. Get off the plane during the stopover and leave the last leg of your journey unused. The airlines frown on this practice, and, of course, you can't check luggage, but you'll save big bucks.

36 BUY ONLY NO-FEE TRAVELERS CHECKS.

If you absolutely feel travelers checks are a must, don't pay a premium for them. Instead, check to see if a credit card issuer, bank or some other membership entitles you to free travelers checks as a benefit.

37 EAT MORE FOR LESS AT YOUR FAVORITE RESTAURANTS.

So you can't kick the restaurant habit. If dining at fine places is your only fiscal vice, that's not so bad. And you can make it—and your credit card statement—better. Ask your favorite places about early-bird and pre-theater specials. Sometimes arriving just half an hour earlier can mean 50% off your food bill. You might also change your eating habits and shift your big meal to lunch. It's better for your health and your wallet since lunch menus are often significantly cheaper.

And if you aren't that hungry, don't shy away from asking for an appetizer as your main course. Finally, don't forget the doggie bag. Even the poshest restaurants no longer sniff at this request. But you should still draw the line at asking for a doggie bag for the unfinished portion of your guest's meal.

38 FREQUENTLY FLY THE NEW UPSTART AIRLINES FOR BIG SAVINGS.

Once again the little guys are giving the long-established players fits. This new breed of airlines has been winning kudos. Check out:

Air South 800-AIRSOUTH	*American TransAir* 800-225-2995
Carnival Airlines 800-824-7386	*Frontier Airlines* 800-432-1359
Horizon Air 800-547-9308	*Kiwi Airlines* 800-538-5494
Leisure Air 800-FLY-WEST	*Markair* 800-627-5247
Midway Airlines 800-446-4392	*Reno Air* 800-RENO-247
SouthWest 800-I FLY SWA	*Tower Air* 800-348-6937
ValuJet 800-825-8538	*Western Pacific* 800-930-3030

General advice: Always use a credit card when you are buying a ticket on a start-up airline. That offers you protection should the airline go out of business. A good general resource is The Worldwide Guide to Cheap Airfares by Michael Wm. McColl (800-78BOOKS or 510-276-1532), $14.

Air South, based in Columbia, S.C., 800-AIR-SOUTH or 803-771-9779. Started in 1994 with $17 million in state and local loans and grants, this carrier has had a tough time keeping on schedule. It just announced a marketing alliance with Kiwi, under which the two will offer joint fares, ticketing and baggage checking. Currently, Air South has 65 departures daily from Columbia, S.C. to Atlanta, Tallahassee, Jacksonville, Miami, Tampa, Myrtle Beach, Raleigh-Durham. Sample fares: $22 per segment.

American TransAir, based in Indianapolis, 800-225-2995 or 317-247-4000. The routes of this charter airline, launched in 1973, change frequently, but along the way it pipes in reggae to its cabins and beverage service includes rum punch and tropical drinks. No Saturday-night stay required and refunds are given up to a week before a flight. Currently, flights are from Indianapolis to Boston, Chicago Midway, Milwaukee, Miami, Sarasota, Tampa, Fort Lauderdale, New York, Los Angeles, St. Thomas, St. Croix and Montego Bay. Also, from Orlando to Albany, Syracuse and Newburgh, N.Y.; Orlando to Providence, Hartford, Cincinnati, Huntsville, Knoxville and Omaha; Chicago Midway to Phoenix, Sarasota, Tampa, Fort Lauderdale, San Juan, St. Thomas, St. Croix and Salt Lake City; and Milwaukee to Phoenix, San Francisco, Los Angeles, Honolulu and Maui, Sarasota, St. Petersburg, Fort Myers, Tampa and Fort Lauderdale. From Boston, it flies to Las Vegas and St. Petersburg.

Airfares: Maximum one-way fare is $149, domestically.

Carnival Airlines, based in Dania, Fla., 800-824-7386 or 305-923-8672. This airline, started in 1988, has 23 planes including Airbus A-300s and Boeing 737s and 727. Service concentrates on fun with in-flight themes like the Bahamas, raffles for prizes and a happy hour in the skies. A roundtrip or advance purchase isn't required to get good fares. And there is no minimum/maximum stay requirement. If you fly 10 roundtrips, you get one free. Routes: Los Angeles to Fort Lauderdale and Miami; Miami to New York; Newark to Nassau; Orlando, Tampa and Fort Myers to Islip, Long Island; Miami to Port-au-Prince, Haiti, and to Punta Cana, Dominican Republic; West Palm Beach to Kennedy; New York and Newark to San Juan, Ponce and Aguadilla, Puerto Rico. Plans are to add, by Christmas, West Palm Beach and Fort Lauderdale to Hartford. Sample fares: West Palm Beach to Kennedy $99 one way; Fort Lauderdale to Los Angeles $149 each way; Fort Lauderdale to Nassau $40 each way; roundtrip New York to Florida $179.

Frontier Airlines, based in Denver, 800-432-1359. This publicly-held startup took off on July 5, 1994 in response to Continental's cuts in service to the Denver hub. Frontier operates a fleet of five 108-seat Boeing 737-200 twin-jets. It has first-class legroom, snacks like oversized muffins and bagels and cream cheese, and mileage credits on Continental Airlines. No Saturday night stay required to get low-fares. It offers one to three flights daily on these routes: Denver to Chicago Midway and Phoenix (3 times daily); Albuquerque, El Paso, Bismarck and Fargo, N.D., Billings, Bozeman, Great Falls and Missoula, Mont.; Las Vegas and Omaha. Sample one-way fares: Denver to Las Vegas $59; Omaha $59; Albuquerque $49; El Paso $59; Bismarck, N.D. $69; Fargo, N.D. $89; Phoenix $59.

Horizon Air, based in Seattle, 800-547-9308. A subsidiary of Alaska Air Group, Inc., Horizon serves 37 cities in Washington, Oregon, Idaho, Montana, California, British Columbia and Alberta. Fares range from $39-$109 each way,

24

requiring a roundtrip purchase and may have other restrictions. Flies from Seattle to Calgary, Portland, Spokane and Boise. From each of those routes, it makes short hops to small cities throughout Washington, Oregon, Idaho, Montana, California, British Columbia and Alberta.

Kiwi International, based in Newark, N.J., 800-538-5494 or 201-645-8445. Former Eastern and Pan Am employees teamed up to create Kiwi. Pilots, who average 20 years' experience, invested $50,000 each while other employees kicked in $5,000. Kiwi has a frequent flyer program, good legroom, advanced boarding and no stay-over restrictions. However, you must book early to get the best fares. Flights are from Atlanta to Newark, N.J. (6 daily), Orlando (6 daily), West Palm Beach (2 daily), Tampa (5 daily), Bermuda (1 daily) and Chicago Midway (4 flights daily). From Newark it flies to Bermuda (1 flight daily), West Palm Beach (2 flights), Orlando (4 flights), Atlanta (4 flights), Tampa (3 flights), Chicago Midway (4 flights).

Sample fares: Lowest restricted fare Atlanta-Chicago $118 roundtrip; Atlanta-Bermuda $393 roundtrip; Newark-Atlanta $228 roundtrip. Walk-ups should expect to pay double.

Midway Airlines, based in Raleigh-Durham, N.C., 800-446-4392 or 919-956-4800. This airline is the ritziest of the low-cost carriers. It has a frequent flyer program with free flights every 10,000 miles, or you can use your miles with American or United. Despite its low-frill cost, Midway has leather seats with extra legroom, light meals and snacks served on china, plus hot towels and mints. Routes are to Boston, Hartford, JFK, Washington, LaGuardia, Islip, N.Y., Newark, Philadelphia, Allentown, Pa., Orlando, Tampa, Fort Lauderdale, Jacksonville and West Palm Beach (3-5 flights a day per destination; fares fluctuate, but sample was $89 roundtrip from Raleigh to LaGuardia; with two weeks advance notice, several routes were $78 roundtrip). Midway is adding San Juan on Oct. 1, 1995.

Reno Air, based in Reno, Nev., 800-RENO-247 or 702-686-3835. This low-fare, full service carrier started July 1, 1992. With 23 MD-80 series jets, Reno is partnered with American Airlines' AAdvantage Travel Awards program. Clean and efficient with a good value in first class, this airline favors 14-day and 7-day advance purchases over walk-ups. Reno offers non-stop service from Reno/Tahoe International Airport to Seattle and Los Angeles. It also flies to San Diego, Orange County, San Jose, Ontario, Portland, Ore., Colorado Springs, Tucson, Lake Tahoe, Las Vegas, Laughlin, Vancouver, British Columbia, Anchorage and Chicago O'Hare. In October, Reno will inaugurate four daily roundtrip flights between LA and Albuquerque and one daily flight to Palm Springs from San Jose. Currently, there are 33 daily flights originating from Reno/Tahoe and 38 daily flights out of its second hub in San Jose. Sample fares: Seattle/San Jose 14-day advance one-way $79/$69; Los Angeles/Reno 21-day advance one way $54; Reno/Chicago (O'Hare) 14-day advance one-way $152.

SouthWest, based in Dallas, 800-I FLY SWA or 214-904-4000. This airline, started in 1971, is the grandaddy of the low-fare, short-hop flights. It serves snacks but no meals. It has a frequent flyer program. Lowest fares require 14-day advance purchase but no overnight stay. SouthWest often fires the first volley that sparks fare wars. It flies to 100 cities. Sample one-way fares: Burbank, LA, Ontario and San Diego to Oakland $49; Sacramento-Seattle $49; Portland-Los Angeles $89; Dallas-Albuquerque $127; Houston-Phoenix $244; Las Vegas-Salt Lake City $69; Chicago-Cleveland $69; Baltimore-Louisville $69; Boise-Phoenix $139; El Paso-Phoenix $139; Tucson-San Diego $69.

Tower Air, based at JFK in New York, 800-348-6937 or 718-553-4300. This airline, which offers longer flights and has no restrictions, typically offers one to five flights daily to its international destinations. Business class only costs $75 (cash only and exact change required) more than coach on most flights. Services Los Angeles, Miami, San Juan, San Francisco, Paris, Israel, Bombay, New Delhi, Sao Paolo, Brazil and Amsterdam. Sample roundtrip fares: NYC-LA $159; NYC-San Francisco $159; NYC-Miami $99; NYC-San Juan $109; NYC-Paris $249; NYC-Amsterdam $199.

ValuJet, based in Atlanta, 800-825-8538 or 404-994-8538. This publicly-owned carrier, started Oct. 26, 1993, is one of the least frilly of the low-cost carriers. Passenger complaints about everything from food to treatment of luggage abound. However, the low prices are hard to beat. All fares are one way and non-refundable. No roundtrip purchase or Saturday night stay is required. Seats are limited. Flies from Atlanta to Louisville, Columbus, Raleigh-Durham, Philadelphia, Hartford, Washington, D.C., Detroit, Chicago, Indianapolis, Nashville, Memphis, Dallas/Fort Worth, New Orleans, Tampa, Savannah, Fort Myers, Jacksonville, Orlando, West Palm Beach, Fort Lauderdale and Miami. From Washington, D.C. to Montreal, Hartford, Chicago, Fort Myers, Jacksonville, Orlando, West Palm Beach, Fort Lauderdale and Miami. Sample fares: 21-day advance purchase Atlanta-Boston $89; Atlanta-New Orleans $49.

Western Pacific, based in Colorado Springs, 800-930-3030 or 719-527-7130. This new startup gives great value on 21-day advance purchases. It flies from Colorado Springs to LA and San Francisco, Oklahoma City, Las Vegas, Phoenix, Chicago Midway, Dallas/Fort Worth, Houston, Indianapolis, Seattle, Wichita and Kansas City ($49-$79 one way); from Dallas-Fort Worth to Colorado Springs, Las Vegas, Los Angeles, Phoenix; San Diego, Seattle and San Francisco; from Houston to Colorado Springs, Las Vegas, Phoenix and San Francisco; from Indianapolis to Colorado Springs, Las Vegas, Phoenix and San

Francisco; from Kansas City to Colorado Springs, Las Vegas, Phoenix, and San Francisco; from Las Vegas to Chicago Midway, Colorado Springs, Dallas-Fort Worth, Houston, Indianapolis, Kansas City, Oklahoma City and Wichita; from Chicago Midway to Colorado Springs, Las Vegas, LA, Phoenix, San Diego, San Francisco and Seattle; Kansas City to Las Vegas, LA, San Francisco (starts at $99 one way); Oklahoma City to Las Vegas ($88 one way).

39 MUSEUMS FOR FREE.

You can view some of the world's greatest art and oddities without paying admission. Most museums in major cities have at least one evening when you can visit their hallowed halls without opening your wallet. In Manhattan, for example, Friday nights are free at such popular museums as the Metropolitan Museum of Art and the Whitney. Other greats include the Boston Museum of Fine Arts and the High Museum in Atlanta. Also, pay attention to those that list a suggested admission. You need only pay what your financial state suggests to you.

40 AIRLINE TICKETS ON THE CHEAP FOR SENIORS.

If you are over 62, Continental Airlines offers Freedom Certificate Booklets that for $999 give you eight one-way tickets to and from anywhere in the continental U.S., good for a year.

41 GOLF AND TENNIS EQUIPMENT BY MAIL FOR BIG SAVINGS.

Las Vegas Discount Golf & Tennis (5325 South Valley Blvd., Las Vegas, Nev. 89119; 702-798-6847) sells brand name equipment at big discounts through a catalog. Send a SASE or the company will quote prices by phone, too.

For racquetball and tennis gear at a 20-40% discount, call mail-order firm Holabird Sports at 410-687-6400, or write 9220 Pulaski Highway, Baltimore, Md. 21220.

42 Restock the Honor Bar in Your Hotel Room.

Don't pay the outrageous prices levied on the bottle of soda or box of peanuts you couldn't resist in your hotel room. Get around it by buying a replacement while you're out. Also, most hotel managers will quickly give in if you protest the excessive charges for items missing from the honor bar.

Also, check your hotel bill for odd charges upon checkout. Some chains have recently been slipping on a $1-2 charge for the safe in your room. Let the hotel know you didn't use it and the desk clerk will remove the charge.

43 Fly Free by Joining Frequent Flyer Clubs.

No matter how infrequently you travel, you might be surprised at how quickly you can rack up enough points for a free flight. First, choose an airline that operates at an airport convenient to you. Ask if it has any other partners—credit card issuers, long distance companies, hotels, rental cars, etc.—and find out the rules for getting points for using those services. Most require you to get 25,000 miles under your belt before you get any free flights. Here are some of the most popular frequent flyer clubs and their phone numbers:

Air Canada: Aeroplan 800-361-8253
Alaska Airlines: Gold Coast Travel 800-654-5669
America West: Fly Fund 800-235-9292
American: AAdvantage 800-882-8880
Continental: One Pass 800-621-7467
Delta: SkyMiles 800-323-2323
Midwest Express: 800-452-2022
Northwest: World Perks 800-447-3757
United: Mileage Plus 800-421-4655
USAir: Frequent Traveler 800-872-4738.

44 FREE INFORMATION ON AIR SAFETY.

If air crashes have you concerned, dial the Federal Aviation Administration's consumer hotline, 800-322-7873, with your questions.

45 FEED THE KIDS ON SOMEONE ELSE'S TAB.

Numerous chains—Boston Market, Bennigan's, Lettuce Souprise You, O'Charleys and Rio Bravo, to name a few—now let children under a certain age eat free on nights that have been traditionally slow. Tuesday seems to be particularly problematic for restaurants. If you're hooked on eating out, take the family on those nights and save 25-50% off your bill. At Boston Market, the meal comes with a show, replete with a clown and free balloons.

46 FREE ADVICE ON HOW TO FIND GOLD.

No fooling. If you think the Gold Rush is over, you're wrong. There are vacation spots where amateur prospectors can still try their hands and their luck. You can get free help by requesting Gold and Prospecting for Gold in the United States, booklets produced by the U.S. Geological Survey Information Services, P.O. Box 25286, Denver, Colo. 80225; 800-435-7627 or 303-236-7477. Dahlonega, a town in the North Georgia mountains, was actually the site of the first gold rush in the U.S. and, for $2, you can pan for gold a block from the town square.

These brochures are just one fun example of the goodies produced by this government group. One of its most requested items is a poster on water, popular with kids. Of course, map lovers will find a treasure trove here. Ask for a list of its publications.

47 GET THE BEST OF YOUR OWN TOWN FREE.

If you live in a town popular with visitors, presumably the main attraction there was what drew you in the first place—be it snow-skiing or golf. The downside is that resorts are usually expensive. Talk to the resort manager about something you can do in exchange for a price break. For example, at Solitude Ski Resort in Salt Lake City (800-748-4754), management gives free season passes (1995 value: $600) to ski hosts, who work a day a week familiarizing guests with the mountain.

Similarly, top-rated family resort Callaway Gardens (800-282-8181) in Pine Mountain, Ga., uses 500 volunteers to act as tour guides, tend its 2,500 acres of land and gardens, or assist in office chores. Volunteers who work only five hours a month receive free season's admission ($30 value) and 30% off at the resort's many restaurants and guest shops.

Consider buying a season's pass to a popular attraction. For a family of four, such a purchase usually pays off after the second visit. One family skipped a $700 charge for a neighborhood swim club and opted instead for a $99 season's pass to a popular water park nearby.

48 IF YOU'RE TRAVELING DURING SUMMER MONTHS, STAY IN A DORM ROOM.

Call 800-525-6633 to order the Budget Lodging Guide, ($14.95 + $2 shipping and handling; B&J Publications, P.O. Box 486, Fullerton, Calif. 92635). This book gives phone numbers for dorms and lodges throughout the U.S. You can get a decent room much cheaper than a hotel.

49 ASK FOR THE BEREAVEMENT FARE IF YOU HAVE TO FLY FOR A FAMILY EMERGENCY.

You don't have to be stuck with a full-fare airline ticket on top of coping with tragedy. Call around to the airlines and ask for bereavement rates, which are often the 7- or 14-day advance rate. You may have to give the name of the doctor at a hospital where your loved one is being treated or the name of the funeral home, but the savings are about 25-50%. The rates also vary from airline to airline. Recently, American Airlines was offering the best deal.

50 Skip Expensive Charges for Excess Airline Baggage.

If you are going on an extended vacation and know you'll be over the airlines' restrictions on luggage, avoid the hefty charges by shipping your belongings to your destination by United Parcel Service (800-742-5877).

51 A Spa Getaway on the Cheap.

Can't afford a week at the Doral Saturnia in Miami? These days there are plenty of options. Extremely popular are one-day urban spas that let you de-stress without a hefty bill to put your neck in knots at the end of your stay. Contact Spa-Finders, a travel agency specializing in spa getaways (800-255-7727). Or you may find one right at your back door. Most large cities have more than a dozen day-spas. Look for spas that offer saunas, steam rooms and hot tubs at no extra charge.

52 Advice on the Best Camp for Your Kid.

Contact the American Camping Association (800-777-CAMP) for its Guide To Accredited Camps ($12.95) to find out what camps in your area are accredited and which ones might best suit your child's needs. A free referral service is the National Camp Association (800-966-2267).

53 Vacation Previews.

Before you spend big bucks to go to a spot that might turn out less than dreamy, consider going there by video. Here are two companies that provide free catalogs of their videos from vacations around the world:

Travaloguer Collection 800-521-5104 (in Colorado call 303-797-9379)

International Video Network 800-669-4486.

54 FREE WINE.

Even if a little dab won't do you, you can at least get a taste of some of the finest wines by stopping in for a wine tour. These days wineries are popping up in parts of the country where they never were found before, so keep your eyes open. For example, Chateau Elan (800-233-WINE or 404-932-0900) in Braselton, Ga., has won more than 200 awards for its wines.

55 GET FREE FUN AT SUPERSTORES.

Visits to malls have seriously dipped and shopping is no longer viewed as recreational sport. However, there are stores that are determined to lure you and your dollars by hook or crook. Barnes & Noble has free story hours twice weekly and play areas for tykes. At Oshman's Super Sports USA (713-967-8365) you can whiz around a 400-ft. track and try out in-line skates, practice your drives at its driving range simulator, wield bow and arrow at its archery range and dribble on its basketball court.

Would-be mountain climbers can test their mettle—and climbing shoes—on rock walls at Recreational Equipment Inc.'s stores (800-426-4840). A visitors' attraction in its own right is the Bass Pro Shop's Outdoor World (417-887-1915) in Springfield, Mo. (Another is soon to be built in Gwinnett County outside Atlanta.) It boasts more than 30,000 sports items, many of which you can try before you buy. An indoor, four-story waterfall feeds into a giant aquarium.

Another good place to get a feel for the sport of your choice is Nike Town (800-344-6453), which has half a dozen stores open across the nation.

56 FREE MOVIES FOR YOUR CHILDREN.

In the interest of promoting community good will, some movie chains offer free movies during the morning hours for your kids. Look for flyers in the late spring, announcing such deals. Also, now that theaters are allowing commercials, watch for offers giving free gifts or discounts for bringing in your ticket stub.

57 FREE OFFICE ON THE ROAD.

Several hotel chains have recently begun providing travelers with free office set-ups in rooms. If you have to take work with you or are traveling on business, request one of these rooms. They typically come equipped with a fax machine, computer hook-ups and multiple-line phone equipped with voice mail. Some hotels will also deliver exercise equipment to your room, free of charge.

58 LAST-MINUTE CRUISE DEALS.

If you keep your bag packed and don't mind vacationing on the spur of the moment, contact one of these agencies:
Cruise Line 800-327-3021
Spur of the Moment Cruises 800-343-1991
Vacations to Go 800-882-9000.

59 GIVE YOUR HOBBY A TEST-RUN.

If you've always dreamed of playing your baby grand, but are dubious about your long-term devotion, check with local piano companies. Some have programs that allow you to rent a piano for a small price like $20 a month and apply rental fees to the purchase price if you decide you've got the stick-to-it-iveness.

Chapter Two

FOUND MONEY

*Check up on your broker, purchase mutual funds for less,
or get a free insurance analysis. It's all for the asking if you
know where to look.*

60 FREE TAX HELP.

You don't have to turn to big-time accountants if your taxes are fairly simple. Instead, call your state's societies of certified public accountants and certified financial planners to find out if either is sponsoring any free help days. These organizations frequently team up with local newspapers or other media to offer assistance.

Or go straight to the source:

IRS Hotline 800-829-1040;

To order tax forms or informational booklets, call 800-TAX-FORM (800-829-3676);

To check on a refund, call 800-829-4477.

The worst times to call these hotlines are Mondays and around lunchtime. Try early in the day, midweek, for the best chance of getting through quickly.

61 GETTING A BEAD ON AN IRS PROFESSIONAL.

If your taxes are complicated, don't take risks. Hire an enrolled agent. These professionals have usually worked for the IRS five years or more, or have passed a test administered by the Treasury Department. The National Association of Enrolled Agents' 24-hour hotline (800-424-4339) provides names of those in your area.

62 FREE GUIDE TO GETTING BIG TAX WRITE-OFFS.

You can turn your company's excess inventory into a tax break and help send a needy kid to college. Call EAL at 708-690-0010 or write P.O. Box 3021, Glen Ellyn, Ill. 60138 for a free guide on where and how to donate your slow-moving inventory for a generous tax write-off. More than 2,000 corporations have participated and helped create college scholarships.

63 NIX STATE OR FEDERAL TAX ON SAVINGS BONDS.

Savings bonds have traditionally been a safe investment. You buy them at half their face value. They give a minimum of 6% interest a year and mature in five years, but they'll continue to accrue interest at a floating rate as long as you hold them—up to 30 years. You never pay state income tax on the interest, and federal tax isn't due till you cash them in. However, now if you buy them in a parent's name and cash them in to pay for college, your interest is exempt from all taxes. Call 800-US-BONDS or contact your local bank for more information.

You can easily track your savings bond portfolio by contacting The Savings Bond Informer (P.O. Box 9249, Detroit, Mich. 48209; 800-927-1901), which will send a free brochure detailing its service (price ranges $12 and up, depending on your holdings). You can also order a copy of U.S. Savings Bonds: A Comprehensive Guide ($24.95) from the company.

64 ADVICE ON MAKING THE MOST OF YOUR 401(K).

You can get free advice from the man who discovered a little-noticed provision in the tax law, which opened the door for the 401(k) in 1980. His name is Ted Benna and he is now the president of The 401(k) Association, One Summit Square, Doublewoods Road and Rte. 413, Langhorne, Pa. 19047, 800-320-401K.

65 A PERSONAL INVESTMENT SERVICE FREE.

If you have $50,000 or more on tap, you can get SteinRoe's Counselor, a personal investment service with no loads or commissions. Call 800-338-2550 for your introductory kit.

66 GO COLD TURKEY AND STOP PAYING 20% FOR THE PRIVILEGE OF BEING IN DEBT.

One of the best ways to make your money go farther is to get control of it in the first place.

A handy book on the topic with tons of useful advice is Andrew Feinberg's Downsize Your Debt ($13, Penguin Books, 800-331-4624). Free counseling is available through some banks, credit unions and employee assistance programs. Other sources include Christian Financial Concepts (800-722-1976) or National Foundation for Consumer Credit (800-388-2227; one-time fee $30). Beware of debt counseling services that charge exorbitant fees. And never fall for services claiming to do credit repair work. These are scam artists looking for a fast buck. Nobody can fix your credit history but you.

67 MONEY EDUCATION.

Get the National Center For Financial Education Money-Book Store Catalog for $1 by sending your name and address to Money-Book Store, P.O. Box 34070, San Diego, Calif., 92163-4070 or call 415-567-5290 or 619-232-8811. This non-profit group has more than 80 money learning and teaching resources—20 of which are geared to kids—and many of which can only be attained through NCFE.

For a free brochure called Selecting a Qualified Financial Planning Professional: Twelve Questions to Consider, call the Institute of Certified Financial Planners' Consumer Assistance line at 800-282-PLAN or write the Institute of Certified Financial Planners, 7600 E. Eastman Ave., Suite 301, Denver, Colo. 80231. Other free brochures are: Your Children's College Bill: How to Figure It, How to Pay for It and Avoiding Investment and Financial Scams.

68 Free Information on Saving More.

April has been declared National Savings Month. Americans aren't saving enough. Merrill Lynch is offering a Family Saving Kit. Call 800-637-7455 ext. SAVE.

69 Track Down the Holes in Your Pockets.

If money seems to slide through your fingers, here's a resource for you: The Budget Kit: The Common Cents Money Management Workbook ($15.95 + $4 shipping and handling; 800-283-4380, Judy Lawrence, P.O. Box 13167, Albuquerque, N.M. 87192).

70 Free 30-Day Trial of WealthBuilder.

When you subscribe to Money magazine, you are entitled to a copy of WealthBuilder ($69.99), personal financial planning software. The package also includes free Prodigy software and one month's usage, a free subscription to Investment Reality newsletter, free trials to more than 25 top investment newsletters and a free month of CheckFree and Bill Pay USA software.

71 Free Contact With a Mortgage Broker.

Mortgage brokers can be heaven-sent for people who are applying for a mortgage but have a few complications: for example, you've recently changed jobs or are self-employed. In that case, mortgage brokers can shop several mortgage deals and come up with the best scenario for your lending situation. To get a referral to some in your area, write the National Association of Mortgage Brokers, 706 E. Bell Road, Phoenix, Ariz. 85022.

72 FREE ADVICE ON THE BEST HOME LOANS.

To keep you from looking for loans in all the wrong places, call HSH Associates at 800-873-2837 or 800-UPDATES. This company specializes in tracking mortgages and trends nationwide. For $20, HSH will send you a listing of lenders with the best rates in your area (updated weekly) and a 42-page booklet, How to Shop for a Mortgage.

73 MAKE SURE YOU AREN'T OVERPAYING INTO YOUR MORTGAGE ESCROW ACCOUNT.

Lenders are notorious for holding more money than necessary in accounts to pay your state tax and insurance expenses. If you think you are being overcharged (escrow should be one-sixth of the amount you'll owe for the year), tell the lender you are considering filing a complaint with the state attorney general's office or bank authority. Most people don't bother to check and therefore lenders get the use of your money, interest free.

If you've been paying for mortgage insurance (demanded by mortgage holders when a homeowner puts less than 20% down on a house), you may be able to quit if you have now paid 20% or more toward the principal. Mortgage companies don't seek you out to let you know that. You have to ask to have that portion of your monthly payment dropped.

74 BUYING OR RENTING?

Which Way to Go? These days that question isn't so simple. A quick and free tip: Generally, if your rent is 65% or less than what a monthly mortgage payment—including property taxes and insurance—would be, stay put. The old rule of a house always making a good investment doesn't hold true.

75 FREE WATCHDOG IF YOU'VE BEEN DISCRIMINATED AGAINST IN HOUSING.

If you've applied for a mortgage, and suspect your age, race or gender had an impact on how you were treated, contact the U.S. Department of Housing and Urban Development's housing discrimination hotline (800-669-9777).

76 SAVE THOUSANDS ON YOUR PROPERTY TAXES.

If you suspect you're paying more than your fair share of taxes on your home or other property, call the tax assessor and ask for information about having your property reassessed. An inspector will be dispatched and your taxes will be lowered. This strategy works well especially in areas like California and the Northeast, where housing prices have been dropping. Conversely, you may be socked with a big increase, but you can still sometimes successfully challenge the assessment.

77 MAKING THE MOST OF REFINANCING.

Even if you missed the historic low interest rates of 1993, refinancing may still make sense at some point. You may be able to lower your monthly payment, shorten your loan time or combine a home equity loan with your new mortgage. Typically, refinancing only makes sense if interest rates are two percentage points lower than your mortgage. For more free information, contact: The Mortgage Bankers Association of America, 1125 15th St. N.W., Washington, D.C. 20005 or 202-861-6500.

One caveat: With the boom in refinancing and new home-buying, hundreds of new mortgage brokers sprang up. They are unregulated, so ask plenty of questions before forking over any money to these outfits.

78 WHOLESALE MORTGAGES.

Who would have thought? If your credit record is top drawer, you may be eligible to get a mortgage from a wholesaler who gives borrowers wholesale rather than retail rates. InfoTrust (610-444-3333) in Kennett Square, Penn., is one such company. Dealing with such a company can save you three-eighths of a percentage or more in interest, which adds up.

79 KEEP MORE IN YOUR POCKET BY PREPAYING YOUR MORTGAGE.

If you won't incur a penalty for doing so, prepay the principal on your mortgage. Paying just an additional $25 a month would save a family paying a $100,000, 30-year mortgage $20,000 in interest, according to Marc Eisenson, author of The Banker's Secret (Box 78, Elizaville, N.Y. 12523; 800-255-0899 or 914-758-1400; $14.95). Order the company's mortgage software ($39.95) to find out what you'd save. As a bonus, you'll get The Consumer's Resource Handbook, which shows you how to resolve every complaint in the book.

80 FREE INFORMATION FOR HOMEOWNERS.

You can get all sorts of free and low-cost help from the non-profit American Homeowners Association (1801 Westport Road, Kansas City, Mo. 64111 or 800-822-3215; $48 annual dues). Membership entitles you to an early mortgage payoff analysis ($1), free CPA advice, educational materials on topics from remodeling to roofing, a quarterly newsletter and an environmental testing kit at cost ($27.36).

81 DON'T OVERPAY ON YOUR ADJUSTABLE-RATE MORTGAGE LOAN.

The formulas that mortgage lenders use to calculate your payments are complicated, and mistakes are easily made. Yet the bank is not going to voluntarily own up to a mistake, especially if it's in your favor. Hire a service to make sure you aren't paying more than you should be once your ARM was adjusted:

Loantech (P.O. Box 3635, Gaithersburg, Md. 20885, 800-888-6781; fee $95) notes that more than half the clients' documents it reviews have been overcharged. Owner David Ginsburg has also launched a service called LoanConsult, which allows you to consult with him or other staff experts about your financing and tax issues. That service costs $2.50 a minute. Some consumers also get a packet of coupons valued at $200 (for a home inspection, lawyers' closing fees, movers and more). For do-it-yourselfers, Ginsberg has written The Homeowner's Escrow Kit ($9.95) and Evaluating Your Adjustable Rate Mortgage ($17.95).

Mortgage Monitor (912 E. Main St., Suite 316, Stamford, Conn. 06902; 800-283-4887) offers a mortgage audit ($99-269) that checks your payments for errors and the escrow account for overcharges. Other products it offers include: the *Homeowner's Property Tax Reduction Kit* ($49.95), the *Mortgage Reducer* ($159) that explains how to pre-pay on your mortgage and a 24-page booklet called Cash In Your Mortgage.

82 CHALLENGE YOUR PROPERTY TAXES.

Tax experts say half of the homeowners who challenge assessments win a reduction of 10% or more. The National Taxpayer's Union publishes How to Fight Property Taxes, a 12-page pamphlet. Send $2 postage and handling to National Taxpayer's Union, Maryland Ave. N.E., Washington, D.C. 20002 or call 202-543-1300.

83 ONE FREE ISSUE OF NEWSLETTERS PACKED WITH MONEY-SAVING TIPS.

Getting goodies for free and cheaply has a chic new appeal. Not surprisingly, several newsletters have sprung up plugging ways to live better on less. Most introductory issues are free, of course. Here are some of the best ones:

The Pocket Change Investor (Good Advice Press, P.O. Box 78, Elizaville, N.Y. 12523; 800-255-0899 or 914-758-1400; quarterly; $12.95 a year);

Cheapskate Monthly (P.O. Box 2135, Paramount, Calif. 90723 or 310-630-8845; one-year subscription: $15.95);

Living Cheap News (7232 Belleview, Kansas City, Mo. 64114; 816-523-3161; 10 issues, $12 a year);

The Penny Pincher (call 800-41PENNY or 516-724-1872 or send $1 and a SASE for a sample to P.O. Box 809-E, Kings Park, N.Y. 11754; monthly; $12 a year);

The Tightwad Gazette (RR 1 Box 3570, Leeds, Maine 04263 or call 207-524-7962; monthly; $12 a year).

84 FREE MONTHLY NEWSLETTERS ON THE ECONOMY.

All 12 Federal Reserve Banks (Altanta, Boston, Chicago, Cleveland, Dallas, Kansas City, Minneapolis, New York, Philadelphia, Richmond and St. Louis) publish free monthly newsletters on economic conditions and financial matters. Write to the one nearest you to be put on a mailing list.

85 GAIN FINANCIAL SAVVY FROM FREE WORKSHOPS.

All the major brokerage firms, some banks, CPA firms and local colleges often sponsor free workshops on topics like estate planning, minimizing taxes and choosing mutual funds. All you have to do is reserve a space. (And you usually get free eats and drinks, too.)

Similarly, the real estate industry continuously sponsors free workshops for first-time homebuyers, on qualifying for a mortgage, how to sell your house and other topics. (Avoid smarmy self-promoters who tout deals that allow you to buy real estate with no money down.) Another good repository of information on seminars is the National Center for Women and Retirement Research (800-426-7386).

86 GET FREE INFORMATION ON (ALMOST) ANY TOPIC.

Don't forget that bastion of free information—Uncle Sam. Mathew Lesko, author of 1,001 Free Goodies and Cheapies (Information USA, P.O. Box 3573, Wallingford, Conn. 06494, 800-862-5372, $19.95) notes the average family pays $10,000 in taxes, yet receives little benefit from that payment. Lesko tells you how to tap into hundreds of free resources. You also get a free audio cassette called Soundbites From History, recorded from famous speeches in the National Archives. Lesko's book—what would you expect?—comes with a 90-day, money-back guarantee.

For instance, want to know something about franchise law? Don't hire a lawyer. Call up the lawyer at the Federal Trade Commission who wrote the book on it. Need demographic information for your marketing plan? Contact your state's data center. For a mere $20 or even free, you can get the best and most up-to-date demographic information available. The National Science Foundation alone has produced more than 3,000 books on health—free for the asking.

The government offers a vast selection of consumer booklets. Everything from the Consumer Handbook on Adjustable Rate Mortgages (50 cents) to How to Buy Surplus Personal Property from the Department of Defense ($1) to How to Find Your Way Under the Hood & Around the Car (50 cents). For the current Consumer Information Catalog, which contains listings for more than 200 free and low-cost government booklets on money, exercise, health, travel, small business and more, contact Consumer Information Center, P.O. Box 100, Pueblo, Colo. 81002 or 719-948-3334.

For free booklets from the Internal Revenue Service, call 800-829-3676. Some recent offerings were its Guide to Free Tax Services, Tax Guide for Small Business and Business Use of Your Home.

If, for example, you have a problem with your landscaping, call the County Agent for a free soil inspection. If an insurance company isn't treating you right, contact your state's insurance commissioner.

If you're a small business owner with a question about exporting or other issues, call the U.S. Small Business Administration (800-827-5722). To find out about product recalls, call the Consumer Product Safety Commission (800-638-2772).

If you're looking for free business advice, the Service Corps of Retired Executives, a federally funded group of retired business executives, stands ready to help entrepreneurs. For the office near you, call 800-634-0245.

87 FIND OUT ABOUT THE BEST CREDIT CARD DEALS.

RAM Research Corporation (800-344-7714 or 301-695-4660; P.O. Box 1700, Frederick, Md. 21702), which produces CardTrak once a month ($5 a copy), does a good job of reporting on the best credit card whether you are looking for a low interest rate, rebate cards or no-fee cards. Even if your wallet is already stuffed full, you may be able to get a better rate and with competition so stiff, some card companies are giving great gifts like vouchers for free airline tickets just for accepting the offer.

88 GET YOUR BANKER TO WAIVE CHECKING FEES.

By maintaining a balance of $1,000 or more in your checking account, you can usually find a banker who will waive the $6-8 monthly checking account fee. A 1993 survey by the American Bankers Association found that more than 70 percent of the nation's commercial banks waived the fees. Look for a bank with average balance requirements rather than minimum daily requirements, or you run the risk of getting sideswiped by the bank. Also, don't keep much more than the minimum required in the account, or you'll lose this game's benefit.

89 UP YOUR VALUE IN THE EYES OF YOUR BANKER.

Combine your accounts with one bank and become a desirable customer. That gives you leverage to get fees waived and reduced. Now most banks and brokerages will include your IRA balances when ranking you as a customer and thereby determining what kind of deal you get on checking and other services.

90 CHEAPER AND SAFER BANKING ALTERNATIVES.

Write the Credit Union National Association, P.O. Box 431, Madison, Wis. 53701, to find out if you're eligible to join a credit union. Service fees are generally lower, they pay better interest rates on your savings and checking accounts, and your money is guaranteed by the National Credit Union Share Insurance Fund, just like the FDIC.

91 $10 FOR PEACE OF MIND.

Before you park big bucks in a bank, check the institution's stability with Veribanc (800-44-BANKS). For $10 (you can charge it), the company will give you the bank's safety rating.

92 SAVE TIME AND MONEY WITH DIRECT DEPOSIT.

Get your paycheck put through on direct deposit. You'll get your money a day earlier and won't have to hassle with lines.

Likewise, you can have most of your utilities automatically deducted from your account. In the long run, it saves you more than $100 each year in postage alone, not to mention the time.

93 USING AUTOMATED TELLER MACHINE CARDS LIKE CHECKS.

With more than 200 million ATM cards in use in the U.S., more and more people are using them in lieu of checks to pay for purchases like gas and food. A new 24-page booklet from MasterCard, titled Shopping With Your ATM Card, explains how to use the new services and where the shopping service networks are in your area. For a free copy, write to the Consumer Information Center, Dept. 36, Pueblo, Colo. 81009.

94 NO-FEE GOLD CARDS.

Although the benefits of carrying a gold credit card are sometimes attractive, most also come with a hefty annual fee ($75 to $100). According to RAM Research (800-344-7714 or 301-695-4660), here are some issuers that offer gold cards with no annual fee:

Amalgamated of Chicago 800-365-6464
AFBA Industrial Bank 800-776-2265
Fidelity Investments 800-323-5353
First Signature Bank & Trust 800-522-1776
Oak Brook Bank 800-666-1011
Union Planters National 800-628-8946.

95 ALMOST FREE ADVICE ON THE BEST CREDIT CARD FOR YOU.

The BankCard Holders of America each month calculates the best cards for consumers with a variety of styles of credit habits. To get a list of low-interest rate cards and no-fee cards, send $4 to BankCard Holders of America, Customer Service, 524 Branch Drive, Salem, Va. 24153 or call 703-389-5445. You can also get information on secured credit cards, if you've had credit problems in the past.

96 FREE INVESTMENT ADVICE IN YOUR MAILBOX.

You can get good information in the form of monthly newsletters sent from your mutual fund companies. Don't dismiss these as so much promotional pablum. In addition, some publishers produce independent newsletters that cover funds. For example, Fidelity Insight (800-638-1987; $99 a year or $39 for four months) concentrates on the Fidelity group of mutual funds.

97 SKIP THE $395 SUBSCRIPTION PRICE FOR MUTUAL FUND SURVEYS AND GO DIRECTLY TO YOUR LIBRARY.

Morningstar Mutual Funds Service (800-876-5005) covers more than 1,300 mutual funds and is the most comprehensive on the topic. Annually, a subscription will cost you $395, but a toll-free call to the company will get you the name of the closest library that offers Morningstar for free. The same goes for Standard & Poor's/Lipper Mutual Fund Profiles (212-208-8000; $132 for four issues a year), which tracks 800 of the largest load and no-load mutual funds.

You can also ask for a free or special introductory rate sample of the proliferation of mutual fund investment newsletters, which can be pricey:

IBC/Donoghue's *Money Letter* 800-445-5900; $89 a year for 24 issues;

InvesTech's *Mutual Fund Advisor and Market Analyst* 800-955-8500 or 406-862-7777; $160 a year for both;

Morningstar *5-Star Investor* 800-876-5005; $79 for a year for the monthly;

Mutual Fund Forecaster 800-442-9000; $49 a year for monthly or five years for $175 gets you five free months and two free books: Stock Market Logic and updates each year of The Buyer's Guide, which features 1,800 mutual funds;

The Mutual Fund Letter 800-326-6941; six-month trial for $39 for six issues or $79 a year;

No-Load Fund Investor 800-252-2042 or 914-693-7420; $119 a year.

Newsletters on emerging stocks include:

Medical Technology Stock Letter 510-843-1857

California Technology Stock Letter 415-726-8495

OTC Insight 510-376-1223.

Select Information Exchange (212-247-7123) offers for $11.95 a package of 20 trial subscriptions that you pick from a list of the most popular. A smart move to make sure you're getting your money's worth if you do decide to subscribe might be to check out the Hulbert Financial Digest (703-683-5905; $37.50 for a five-issue trial subscription; or $67.50—half-price—for a first-time subscriber for a year), which keeps tabs on 170 investment newsletters, tracks their recommendations and rates their performances.

98 INSIDER'S INFORMATION ON MUTUAL FUNDS.

Contact the Mutual Fund Investors Association, 20 William St., Suite G-70, P.O. Box 9135, Wellesley Hills, Mass. 02181-9415 or call 800-444-6342. Request a free copy of Fidelity Profit Alert.

99 FREE HELP WITH YOUR MUTUAL FUNDS.

Fidelity FundMatch (800-282-3116) gives a free worksheet and workbook that help investors figure out a personal investment strategy.

100 SAVE FEES BY USING DISCOUNT BROKERS TO PURCHASE NO-LOAD MUTUAL FUNDS.

Discount brokerages have been slashing fees right and left. You can use them to purchase hundreds of no-load mutual funds (like T. Rowe Price International Stock Fund 800-547-7684 or Janus 800-525-8983) and wind up paying extremely low fees— saving as much as 60%. These days, discounters perform almost all the functions a full-service brokerage does—even producing a version of an assets management account made popular by Merrill Lynch. You can have an account with free checking, a VISA or MasterCard tied to your money market account, and a convenient statement each month. Yet, once again you'll pay about one-third of price for the privilege. (Merrill Lynch's Cash Management Account fee is $100 a year.)

Below are some of the biggest firms:

Charles Schwab 800-648-5300

Fidelity Discount Brokerage Services 800-544-8666

Jack White & Co. 800-223-3411 or 800-323-3263

Muriel Siebert & Co. 800-872-0666

Olde Discount 800-USA-OLDE

Quick & Reilly 800-926-0600

Waterhouse Securities 800-934-4443.

101 FREE CHECK-UP FOR YOUR STOCKBROKER.

Want to find out if your broker has any black marks on his or her record? Call the National Association of Securities Dealers (800-289-9999) and ask if there have been any disciplinary actions taken against the broker by state or federal regulators. If so, NASD will send you the details at no charge. So call before you put your financial future in a broker's hands.

102 Buy Stocks but Skip the Commission.

Relatively few companies allow you to make a direct investment in their shares sans broker. However, here are a few: AmeriRecreation Centers, Atlantic Energy, Bancorp Hawaii, Dominion Resources, Duke Power, Exxon, First Alabama Bancshares, Florida Progress, Hawaiian Electric, Johnson Controls, Madison Gas & Electric, Minnesota Power & Light, New Jersey Resources, Oklahoma Gas & Electric, SCANA Corp. Union Electric, WICOR and Wisconsin Energy.

Almost 1,000 companies offer dividend reinvestment plans (DRIPs) through which you can automatically reinvest dividends at little or no commission and bypass your broker after your initial purchase. No wonder brokers don't want you to know about DRIPs.

103 A Guide to Freebies for Stockholders.

Grab a copy of Free Lunch on Wall Street by Charles B. Carlson (McGraw-Hill, $14.95) at the library.

This book gives you all sorts of ideas on how to get freebies when you purchase stock, from 10% off weekend lodging if you own Marriott stock to 3-5% discounts on shares purchased through dividend reinvestment plans.

104 Free Annual Reports.

You can get free annual reports first-class mail through a reader service program with The Wall Street Journal by calling 800-654-CLUB and requesting any company that has the club symbol by its name on the ticker pages. This solution is much more timely than calling the investor relations department of the company directly—and less costly.

105 GIVE STOCKS THAT COME WITH FREE GIFTS.

Several stocks come with an extra sweetener that makes giving a share or two extra fun. For example, Wrigley sends out 20 packs of chewing gum to shareholders each December. Owning just one share of Disney, another example, gets you a discounted membership ($50) in the Magic Kingdom Gold Club (407-352-3207). That entitles you to 10-30% discounts at Walt Disney resorts, attractions, stores in malls, and 10% off airfare if you fly Delta to Orlando.

You can avoid commissions on an odd lot by buying stocks direct from some companies. Many companies— Mattel, Coca-Cola and McDonald's, to name a few—have dividend reinvestment plans that allow you to sidestep costly brokerage commissions.

Some mutual funds are geared to the younger set, too. SteinRoe's Young Investor Fund (800-322-2550) comes with a packet of material including a booklet on saving and a wall chart upon which the mini-mogul can chart the fund's performance. Those 18 (or 21, depending on the state) and younger are eligible. They'll also get a quarterly newsletter called Dollar Digest. You can open a custodial account with as little as $1,000.

106 GET FREE FINANCIAL ADVICE.

Some organizations produce outstanding booklets on important topics like mortgages, banks, credit and more. Here are some great resources: The Consumer's Almanac (American Financial Services Association, Consumer Credit Education Foundation, 919 18th St. N.W., Suite 300, Washington, D.C. 20006 or 202-296-5544); for more than 20 terrific publications including the Low Rate, No Fee Credit Card List, Secured Credit Card List, Managing Family Debt and Getting Out of Debt (BankCard Holders of America, 524 Branch Drive, Salem, Va. 24153 or 703-389-5445), and a newsletter called

The Safe Money Report (Weiss Research, 4176 Burns Road, Palm Beach Gardens, Fla. 33410, 800-289-9222 or 407-627-3300).

For some of the best financial information for children and adults, get a free catalog from the National Center for Financial Education (800-837-5729).

107 FOLLOW YOUR STOCKS WITHOUT PAYING A BUNDLE.

Brokerage firms and libraries carry the Value Line Investment Survey and Standard & Poor's Stock Reports. For more detailed reports, you can purchase an 8-10 page comprehensive report on a company from Standard & Poor's (800-847-0342 for $9.95). If Fidelity is your brokerage, you can get discounted reports for $5.95 each.

108 GET FREE INVESTMENT ADVICE FROM AN INVESTMENT CLUB.

The National Association of Investments Corporation (810-583-6242 or fax 810-583-4880) sends out reams of information on how to form a club, set up accounting procedures and create a partnership agreement, if you ask. Then, if you join, dues are only $30 per club plus $10 a member. For that price, you get more advice, plus the monthly Better Investing magazine. Being in a club gives you access to investment experts who will gladly come and speak at your meetings. You also have the benefit of your peers' experience and legwork.

109 MORE INVESTMENT ADVICE AT A LOW, LOW RATE.

If you are a maverick investor, you still may want to link up with the American Association of Individual Investors (312-280-0170; $49 annual dues). For that price you get tax and financial planning booklets in December, 10 issues of its journal and a book called The AAII Guide to No-Load Mutual Funds, updated annually in March.

110 Free Shareholders Meetings.

Okay, so they may not be the snazziest in terms of entertainment, but you can learn a lot about a company by attending a shareholders meeting. Where and when the meeting will be held is found in the company's 10K or you can call the investor relations department of the company that has captured your interest. Companies sometimes provide free surprise gifts for attendees—although typically they aren't lavish, so as not to alarm the stockholders in the crowd. And you do not have to be a shareholder to attend. Also, don't take it for granted the shareholders meeting will be in the town in which the company is headquartered. Companies often move their meetings around and have them in unexpected places. For example, Coca-Cola, headquartered in Atlanta, usually holds its meeting in Wilmington, Del.

111 Get Checks for Less.

Those little savings add up quickly. Order checks for business or personal use at half the cost of the bank's charges. Compare prices of The Current, Inc. (P.O. Box 19000, Colorado Springs, Colo. 80935; 800-533-3973); Checks in the Mail (P.O. Box 7802, Irwindale, Calif. 91706, 800-733-4443); The Check Store (P.O. Box 5145, Denver, Colo. 80217-5145, 800-424-3257); U.S. Response (P.O. Box 1037, Bedford, Texas 70590, 800-880-0906 or 817-355-9696); or Artistic Checks (P.O. Box 1501, Elmira, N.Y. 14902, 800-224-7621 or 607-733-9010).

112 Ask for Return of Deposits on Utilities.

If you've lived in your present residence a year or more, you are entitled to have your deposits returned. But most companies don't bother unless you ask. So do it today. You might also want to check with the state treasury where you used to live.

Abandoned utility deposits sometimes wind up in the state's coffers and little is done to track down the rightful owner. You may have a small fortune awaiting you.

113 CHEAP ADVICE FOR DRIP INVESTORS.

For more information on buying stock directly from companies, call First Share ($12 annual membership fee) at 800-683-0743. The National Association of Individual Investors ($32 annual membership), 1515 East Eleven Mile Road, Royal Oak, Mich. 48067, also offers a low-cost investment plan with more than 100 companies.

114 BUY U.S. TREASURY OFFERINGS DIRECTLY AND AVOID BROKERAGE FEES.

Although brokers will be happy to sell U.S. Treasury Bonds to you, you can buy them commission-free directly from the Bureau of Public Debt, Washington, D.C. 20239 or call Treasury Direct Purchasing Information at 202-874-4000.

115 TRACK YOUR SAVINGS BONDS.

The government provides free tables that allow you to track your savings bond's performance. However, they can be difficult to decipher. Another solution: You can pay the Savings Bond Informer (800-927-1901; P.O. Box 9249, Detroit, Mich. 48209 for a free brochure on the service) to keep tabs on your holdings. You are charged according to a graduated scale and how many bonds you have. For example, if you held 1-10 bonds, you'd be charged $12; 301-500 bonds, you'd pay $49. Fifty-five million Americans hold bonds, more than any other security, yet there is little information easily available on them. You can also order U.S. Savings Bonds: A Comprehensive Guide by Dan Peterson from the company for $24.95.

116 DO-IT-YOURSELF CREDIT REPAIR.

Avoid so-called credit repair clinics. Nobody can take care of a besmirched credit record but you. A first step may be to reestablish credit. Many lending institutions will let you open an account and draw against that secured account. RAM Research (P.O. Box 1700, Frederick, Md. 21702) give the names of 100 reputable banks that issue secured credit cards. Call 800-874-8999 and ask for "Secured Credit Card Report 1995" ($10). Here are some secured card issuers:

American Pacific Bank 800-879-8745

Citibank (South Dakota) 800-743-1332

Key Federal Savings Bank 800-228-2230.

117 FREE CONSUMER CREDIT COUNSELING.

Likewise, beware of scam artists eager to "help" you rebuild a sullied financial rating. Legitimate help comes from:

Family Service America, Inc., 11700 West Lake Park Drive, Milwaukee, Wis. 53224; 800-221-2681;

The National Foundation for Consumer Credit, 8611 Second Ave., Silver Spring, Md. 20910;

800-388-2227.

These non-profits will refer you to a local counselor who will advise you on getting back on solid ground and will even contact creditors for you to facilitate a payment plan.

118 A FREE FINANCIAL MAKEOVER.

Mary Hunt, author of Cheapskate Monthly, found her family $100,000 in debt in 1983, largely due to her own out-of-control spending. She is a recovered shopaholic who went on to found, with her husband, a successful commercial real estate venture. She started her newsletter, believing that others could profit (and save) from the lessons she learned on the way to digging out from under that debt. Hunt offers free information on a do-it-yourself financial makeover. Write Financial Makeover, c/o Cheapskate Monthly, P.O. Box 2135, Paramount, Calif. 90723-8135 or call 310-630-8845. Send a business-sized SASE with the words "Financial Makeover" printed in the lower left-hand corner.

119 SKIP THE FRONT-END SALES COMMISSION ON INTERNATIONAL STOCKS.

Here are several international stock funds that don't charge sales commissions (usually 6% or less):

Fidelity Europe Fund 800-544-8888
Fidelity Worldwide Fund 800-544-8888
Financial Strategic European 800-525-8085
Financial Strategic Pacific Basin 800-525-8085
Japan Fund 800-535-2726
Nomura Pacific Basin 800-833-0018
Scudder International Fund 800-225-2470
T. Rowe Price European Stock 800-638-5660
T. Rowe Price International Stock Fund 800-638-5660
T. Rowe Price New Asia 800-638-5660
Twentieth Century International Equity 800-345-2021
Vanguard International Equity Index European 800-662-7447
Vanguard World International Growth 800-662-7447
Vanguard International Equity Index Pacific 800-662-7447.

120 GETTING THE MOST FOR YOUR DOLLAR OVERSEAS.

Do not exchange money at airports or hotels. Instead, for the best rate, exchange travelers checks in U.S. dollars to the foreign currency in small amounts as you need it. (Exception: If the U.S. dollar is falling like a rock, purchase in the currency of your destination country.) Converting back to U.S. currency is often fairly expensive, so try to avoid needing to do so. Another way to get a more favorable rate is to take cash from an automatic teller machine. Overseas, that rate is often the best around. However, just be sure your PIN number will work in the country to which you are traveling. Check with your card issuer before departure.

121 FREE GUIDANCE TO THE NEAREST CASH MACHINE.

Stuck in a strange town without cash? Help is only a toll-free call away. For American Express, dial 800-CASH NOW. For Discover, call 800-347-2683.

122 GET AN ASSET MANAGEMENT ACCOUNT AT A BROKERAGE HOUSE.

For some, an account that rolls checking, stock trades, a credit/debit card and more all into one convenient statement may actually be less costly than maintaining a checking, savings and other accounts at a bank by the time you add in all the fees.

Now several brokerage houses (including discounters) have asset management accounts that allow you to write checks and use them as you would a bank. Merrill Lynch pioneered the concept with its Cash Management Account (cost: $100; $20,000 minimum; 800-CMA-INFO). A CMA account gives you unlimited free checking, daily interest on cash balances, automatic direct deposit of payroll, pension or Social Security checks, free Visa debit card, Merrill Lynch stock research and the stock brokerage. The Fidelity Ultra Service Account (cost: no annual fee; $5,000 minimum; 800-544-6262) gives you all the same benefits, with the exception, of course, of stock research. Your account is still insured up to $100,000 with the FDIC.

123 A LOW-COST SEARCH FOR TAX-DEFERRED GUARANTEED-RATE ANNUITIES.

Another investment choice that you don't have to pay taxes on until you take the money out is a guaranteed-rate annuity.

Insurance companies pay you a guaranteed interest rate on your investment. There is no commission charged up-front on most of these (although it is built into the price overall). Here are two sources that will provide you low-cost help to make the wisest choice: First, check the insurance company's stability with Weiss Research at 800-289-9222. From there you can either call several insurance companies on your own to compare the percentage they are offering or use Independent Advantage Financial Services, an annuity shopping service. Call 800-829-2887 and ask for its free honor roll of guaranteed-rate annuities, which compares the characteristics of six top companies' annuities.

Another option that makes annuities less expensive is to buy through mutual fund managers. Expense charges tend to be slightly lower, and you may not have a surrender charge (a penalty for getting out of the investment within the first five years or so). Mutual fund companies that sell annuities directly include:

Fidelity 800-544-0140
Scudder 800-225-2470
Vanguard 800-522-5555.

124 ALMOST $10 BILLION SITS IN STATES' UNCLAIMED PROPERTY.

If you are the beneficiary of a deceased person or even think you may have neglected to give your address to an institution holding stocks or other valuables in your name, contact your state's abandoned property department by phone or mail. Give your name (or former name), your Social Security number, current address and all previous addresses while living in that state to help the appropriate agency make a match. If a windfall is being held in your name, you'll be sent a claim form. Tip: If a company contacts you offering to help you locate funds, you can rest assured that there is a nice sum awaiting your call. Bypass the finder's fee and grab the goods yourself.

125 A Cheap Way to Play the Index.

If you want to invest in the S&P 500 Stock Index, an inexpensive route is the United Services All-American Equity Fund (800-873-8637), which will let you open an account for as little as $100 if you open an "ABC" account. That means you let the company withdraw as little as $30 a month from your account. Other indexes are:

Fidelity Market Index Fund 800-544-8888

Vanguard Index Trust 500 Portfolio 800-662-7447.

If you desire great diversity in your portfolio without hiring a financial planner or adviser, consider two no-load mutual funds that do all the work for you:

Fidelity Asset Manager 800-544-8888

Vanguard Star Fund 800-662-7447.

126 Free Help for Your Personal Savings and Loan Crisis.

If you're having a problem with your savings and loan, contact the U.S. Office of Thrift Supervision, Consumer Programs, 1700 G St. N.W., Washington, D.C. 20552 for a a free Guide to Consumer Assistance. It will explain the procedures you'll need to follow to complain and get help.

127 Lawyer in a Box.

In some states, you can take care of common legal transactions using software and boilerplate documents. For instance, to write even a simple will, a lawyer would charge $300 and up. You could do your own for one-tenth the cost using your computer. The cheapest do-it-yourself law software programs include:

It's Legal ($29 + $5 shipping and handling;
    800-223-6925; Parsons Technology—also produces
    Personal Home Inventory, $19)

Personal Law Firm ($49.95 + $6.50 shipping and
   handling; 800-833-8082)
Willmaker ($55.96 + $4 shipping and handling;
   800-992-6656; Nolo Press).

128 GET LEGAL HELP FOR 50% LESS.

Have a legal wrangling in the works? Tapping into arbitration
could save you as much as 50%. Going to court can be extremely costly. But you can get justice for less by using these resources:
American Arbitration Association, 140 W. 51st St., New
York, N.Y. 10020; 212-484-4000.
American Bar Association's Standing Committee on Dispute
Resolution, 1800 M St. N.W., Washington, D.C. 20036; 202-
331-2258. This committee has a directory of numerous low-
cost mediation programs across the country.
The local chapter of Better Business Bureau or
the National Council of Better Business Bureaus at 800-537-
4600 for local dispute resolution programs.

   There are also several private alternative dispute resolution
firms that will help with legal mires:
Judicial Arbitration & Mediation/Endispute Services
800-352-5267 or 235 Peachtree St., Suite 600,
Atlanta, Ga. 30303.
Washington Arbitration 800-933-6348.

   Although prepaying for legal services continues to be a growing industry, most consumer experts warn against them. This
"bargain" on the surface really doesn't buy you much, and it's one
deal you don't need.

129 USE SMALL CLAIMS TO GET BIG DOLLARS.

If you've got a legitimate beef with an individual or business,
consider getting your due in small claims court. A lot of folks
don't realize how cheap and easy filing a claim is: It's usually

less than $100, which you'll recover if you win, and you don't have to hire a lawyer. The clerk of the court in the country where you file usually gives you a free information kit to assist you. Tip: Read Everybody's Guide to Small Claims Court by Ralph Warner (Nolo Press; $18.95 + $4 shipping and handling; 800-992-6656).

130 SLASH LEGAL COSTS.

Yes, there are ways to get around out-of-control legal costs. Here are some great resources: 100 Ways to Cut Legal Fees and Manage Your Lawyer by Erwin Krasnow and Robin Conrad. Send $10.95 plus $1 shipping to the National Chamber Litigation Center, 1615 H St. N.W., Washington, D.C. 20062 or call the U.S. Chamber of Commerce to order at 800-638-6582.

Another good book is Small Claims Court: Making Your Way through the System ($8.95 + $1.80 shipping and handling; Sarah Parker Publications). Order through HALT: An Organization of Americans for Legal Reform, 1319 F St. N.W., Suite 300, Washington, D.C. 20004; 202-347-9600.

To go to the source, you might also try the American Bar Association's guide, The American Lawyer: When and How to Use One ($4.50; 312-988-5522).

The following firms specialize in auditing legal bills, which are sometimes padded:

Law Audit Services 203-221-2810

Legalgard 800-525-3426

Stuart, Maue, Mitchell & James 314-291-3030.

131 GET A FREE ANALYSIS OF YOUR HOMEOWNER'S AND AUTO INSURANCE.

In the wake of all the hurricanes, tornadoes, floods, earthquakes and fires in recent years, checking up on your homeowner's policy would be wise. Make sure you have guaranteed replacement cost insurance. That means that the insurer must pay for what it would cost to replace your belongings and rebuild your home exactly as it was at today's construction prices. A common mistake in overinsuring: Only insure the cost of the building and your belongings. Don't pay to insure the land it's on.

Take an inventory complete with video and serial numbers. Make a copy and keep it someplace other than your house. As several homeowners in California discovered the hard way, insurers won't pay up if you can't prove you owned items. With valuable antiques or art, have a professional appraisal done. Otherwise, you'd only get the replacement value of an old chair, for instance ($20 or so), vs. what you would get for a solid cherry Victorian rocker dating to 1860.

Also, if you work from home and see clients there, you may be underinsured. Policies have strict outlines on what they'll pay regarding computers and other equipment, plus you may not have enough liability insurance. Check with your agent on special riders that can be purchased.

Remember that flooding is not covered on homeowners' policies. You have to purchase flood insurance separately from the government—although your agent should be able to handle the paperwork for you. Also, if a flood is even a remote possibility, contact the Federal Insurance Administration and ask about the National Flood Insurance Program (800-638-6620). For the $200-500 a year it costs, you've got a good deal.

A recent study showed that more than 30% of homes are underinsured, primarily because so many people now have home offices equipped with computers and such that are not covered. Call your insurance agent and get a free re-evaluation to help determine if your needs are being met. Scan the policy to find out if you're paying for benefits you don't need—like insurance on jewelry and furs. Being overinsured is a big money-waster, too, because insurance companies won't pay off beyond what they determine is a fair amount for the actual value of your belongings or home. Some companies insure what you paid for your home, but your land should not be included in the homeowner's policy. The land your home is built on wouldn't have to be rebuilt, yet millions of home-owners are paying on the purchase cost of their home, rather than the actual replacement value of it.

132 INSURANCE SAVERS.

Stop collision coverage on older cars that aren't worth it. Consider raising deductibles on both your home and car insur-ance. Putting in small claims can cause you big trouble. (Insurers will often cancel you if you have two claims in the same year—even if they aren't your fault.) If you have extensive assets and some risks—for example, a teenage driver in the fam-ily—an umbrella policy may save you from financial ruin in these days of big jury awards. For small premiums, an umbrella policy gives you coverage over and above what is customary.

To lower insurance costs:

Raise your deductible. Putting in small claims could cause you to lose your insurance anyway. Most commonly, your agent will offer a $250 deductible. Increase it to $1,000 and save about 15%. (Check with your mortgage lender, though. Some won't allow you to have more than a $500 deductible.)

Shop around. This business is extremely competitive, so take advantage of it.

Lower premiums by improving your odds. Some insurers give better rates to residences that have several smoke alarms, a burglar alarm and a house full of non-smokers.

Ask for a decrease. If you've been with the same company several years without making claims, ask for a good-customer reduction.

Give all your business to the same insurer. If you combine your auto policy business with your homeowner's, your insurer may be willing to give you a discount as well.

133 FREE INSURANCE ADVICE AND TIPS.

Disputes over insurance can be costly. Get your questions answered by calling the National Insurance Consumer Helpline (800-942-4242). Sponsored by the Insurance Information Institute, the hotline will send out dozens of free pamphlets that untangle the sticky web of insurance lingo. One of the most requested is 12 Ways to Lower Your Homeowner's Insurance.

A free booklet called The Consumer's Guide to Health Insurance is available by writing the Health Insurance Association of America, 1025 Connecticut Ave. N.W., Washington, D.C. 20036. The American Council of Life Insurance, 101 Pennsylvania Ave. N.W., Washington, D.C. 20004-2599 (202-624-2000) produces a free, 12-page brochure called What You Should Know About Buying Life Insurance.

134 NIX INSURANCE YOU DON'T NEED.

Buying insurance is tricky enough, and insurers are anxious to part you from your money. Here are insurance policies you don't need:

Accidental Death Insurance. Statistically, this insurance is a waste.

Child Life Insurance. Of course, your little darling is precious but your money would be better invested in a savings bond, zero coupon bond or some other item.

Extended Warranty Coverage. First of all, the price of electronics, computers and other gadgetry has been dropping with regularity. By the time you could possibly use this contract, it would probably have been cheaper to buy the item in question new. Plus, these are rarely used.

Mortgage Insurance. Your regular life insurance should be sufficient to pay off the mortgage. The other drawback is that the potential benefit decreases as you pay down your principal, yet the premium on this insurance remains the same.

Travel Insurance. This expensive insurance peddled at airports is often a free benefit if you charge your airline ticket to a premium credit or charge card. And besides, you don't need it.

135 BUY DISABILITY INSURANCE DIRECT FROM THE INSURER.

Disability insurance has gotten cheaper in the last few years, but is still pricey. Shop around and get quotes from at least five insurers. To save the agent's commission, check with the USAA Life Insurance Company (9800 Fredericksburg Road, San Antonio, Texas 78288; 800-531-8000 ext. 83322). It allows you to buy directly.

136 SAVE OVER THE LONG HAUL BY USING AN INSURANCE-BUYING SERVICE OR ADVISER.

If you own a small to medium-sized business or have significant assets to cover, there are a handful of fee-only advisers who can give you advice on how to best protect your assets. Here are several services that offer more detailed help in the confusing world of life insurance policies:

Life Insurance Advisors Association (President Peter Katt, Katt & Co., 2822 Bay Drive, West Bloomfield, Mich. 48324; 800-521-4578 or 810-360-4468; $195 an hour). Katt is the author of The Life Insurance Fiasco and How to Avoid It ($19.95; self-published) and manages a $300 million portfolio of life insurance for his clients.

Assured Enterprises, Ltd. (600 West Jackson, 8th Fl., Chicago, Ill. 60661; 800-701-0898 or 312-993-0355) charges $150 an hour for advice. Write for a free copy of owner Ted Bernstein's Life Insurance Buying Guide.

Fee for Service (5401 West Kennedy Blvd., Suite 560,

Tampa, Fla. 33609; 800-874-5662) also charges $150 an hour for advice.

Insurance Information Inc. (800-472-5800; 23 Route 134, South Dennis, Mass. 02660) is an independent shopping service—it does not sell insurance—that will give you the five lowest priced term life policies for your age and sex for a $50 fee. Life insurance should be six times your annual salary.

137 GET THE BEST DEAL ON AUTO INSURANCE.

Prices for coverage vary dramatically in this category: in some states as much as 100%. So shopping around is critical. Also, you may get discounts for the following: insuring multiple cars; good driving record; paying premiums annually rather than quarterly or monthly; installing anti-theft devices; having anti-lock brakes and airbags; student discounts for those with good grades or taking a driver's education course and senior drivers with good driving records.

138 KEEP TRACK OF CAR TAX DEDUCTIONS.

Take a small notebook and leave it in your car. Make it a habit to jot down the date and mileage whenever you're driving for business (29 cents per mile). What you may not know is that you can also deduct 12 cents per mile for volunteer work, and 9 cents a mile for doctor visits. At the end of each month, tally the total to encourage you to keep it up.

139 FREE HELP TO TEACH YOUR KIDS ABOUT MONEY.

Send a SASE to Consumer Federation of America (CFA, 1424 16th St. N.W., Suite 604, Washington, D.C. 20036) for a free brochure titled Teaching Your Child How to Save and Spend. CFA is a federation of 240 consumer groups.

140 Get the Highest Yield on a CD.

If you have a large amount you'd like to put in a CD, call 100 Highest Yields (407-627-7330; $20 for four weeks or $124 for a year). This weekly publication surveys the highest-yielding CDs and money market accounts and gives subscribers toll-free numbers to contact. With interest rates on the rise again, you're more likely to find bigger spreads. You can easily purchase a federally insured CD by mail. But taking the time to do this extra homework only makes sense for a large nest egg. Otherwise, stick to your hometown.

141 Sidestep State Income Taxes on Money Market Funds.

Here are some funds that only invest in short-term U.S. Treasury securities:

Capital Preservation Fund (800-4-SAFETY)
Dreyfus 100% U.S. Treasury Fund (800-242-8671)
T. Rowe Price U.S. Treasury Money Market Fund (800-638-5660)
United Services Treasury Securities Cash Fund (800-873-8637).

142 Get the Real Deal on Long Distance Services.

The war between the long distance companies blazes hotter and hotter and you the customer stand to benefit. To know how the services measure up where you are concerned, get expert advice from the non-profit Telecommunications Research and Action Center (TRAC), 202-462-2520. TRAC does a cost-comparison service for small businesses ranging from $100 a month in long distance charges to more than $6,000. For a copy of Tele-Tips Small Business, send $5 and a SASE to TRAC, P.O. Box 12038, Washington, D.C. 20005. Also available for $3 and a SASE from TRAC is Tele-Tips Residential Chart. Or to find a telephone consultant, contact the Society of Telecommunications Consultants, 13766 Center St. Suite 212, Carmel Valley, Calif. 93924, or 800-782-7670; fax 408-659-0144.

143 Low-Cost Estate Planning Advice.

Estate Planning Specialists (800-223-9610) gives you a complete estate analysis and recommends living trusts, insurance trusts and other tax-saving strategies, for a $69 fee. The group will also refer you to a local lawyer specializing in estate planning.

144 Find an Elder Law Attorney for Free.

If you have an older relative whose care has fallen on your shoulders, contact the National Academy of Elder Law Attorneys, Inc. (1604 North Country Club Road, Tucson, Ariz. 85716; 602-881-4005 or fax 602-325-7925) for a free referral to a lawyer specializing in elder law in your area. Laws vary widely from state to state, so having a lawyer who is up-to-date is important.

145 Befriend the Internal Revenue Service and Get a Cut From Tax Cheats.

If you can prove that someone you know is cheating on his or her income taxes, give the IRS the appropriate information and you could get 10% (up to $100,000) of the back taxes collected by the U.S. government. All you have to do is fill out a form. Call 800-829-3676.

146 Make Small Cuts on Your Regular Bills.

Evaluate your cable bill to make sure you aren't paying for a service you aren't using much. Consider nixing the wire protection charge on your telephone bill. It's essentially $2 a month insurance against you having a wiring problem inside your house—something that is extremely unlikely to happen. Nix call waiting. This service is expensive and should you have a true emergency, the operator can always break in. If you really can't afford to miss calls, use voice mail instead. Pay attention to your water bill. Even a small increase can indicate a slow leak in your system. Quickly investigate.

147 GET THE BEAD ON YOUR SOCIAL SECURITY NEST EGG.

Wondering how much Uncle Sam has socked away on your behalf? You can find out for free. Request a free Personal Earnings and Benefit Statement from Social Security (800-772-1213). It'll outline your entire work history, tell you how much you'll get at 62 or your entitlement and your dependents' if you were disabled. Keeping tabs on the government never hurts. If you find a mistake, let the Social Security folks know immediately.

148 SHOP FREE FOR EXPERT FINANCIAL ADVICE.

When you're seeking a professional to handle your finances, don't proceed on blind faith. If someone is claiming to be a certified financial planner, you can quickly check his or her credentials by calling the Certified Financial Planners Board of Standards (303-830-7543). This organization won't recommend one for you, but can tell you if the person has actually completed the required courses to earn the designation.

For no charge, the Institute of Certified Financial Planners (800-282-7526) will send you a biography and information on certified financial planners in your area. The International Association for Financial Planning (800-945-IAFP or 404-395-1605) will also provide you with such a list. For a list of financial planners who charge a flat fee rather than commissions on products they sell, contact the National Association of Personal Financial Advisors (800-366-2732 or 708-537-7722).

149 Skip Extended Service Contracts...

Period. Save yourself a bundle. Never buy one of these babies—especially on appliances and small electronics. It rarely pays for you.

150 Buy No-Load Ginnie Mae Mutual Funds.

Skip commissions and get a lower cost by buying these mortgage-backed securities:

Benham GNMA Income 800-472-3389
Dreyfus GNMA 800-645-6561
Fidelity Ginnie Mae 800-544-8888
Franklin U.S. Government 800-342-5236
Scudder GNMA 800-225-2470
T. Rowe Price GNMA 800-638-5660
Vanguard Fixed-Income GNMA 800-662-7447.

No-load government-insured adjustable rate mortgage funds include:

Benham Adjustable Rate Government Securities Fund
800-472-3389
T. Rowe Price Adjustable Rate U.S. Government Fund
800-638-5660
Value Line Adjustable Rate U.S. Government Securities Fund
800-223-0818.

151 Make Sure Your Life Insurer, HMO and Bank Are Fiscally Fit.

Remember the savings and loan crisis? Weiss Ratings, Inc. (4176 Burns Road, Palm Beach Gardens, Fla. 33410; 800-289-9222 or 407-627-3300) will send you a report on your life insurer, your HMO, your bank or your S&L, for $15 each, which can be charged. If you want even more detail, you can get an 18-page Personal Safety Report on your insurance company for $45. Weiss has developed a reputation for being much tougher on companies than some of the older ratings companies.

152 FREE RETIREMENT GUIDE.

Several brokerage firms and other folks offer such retirement planning guides. They only require a toll-free call. An especially good one is the T. Rowe Price Retirement Planning Kit (800-638-5660). Another to order is Retirement Made Easy, a free brochure from Aetna (800-AETNA60).

153 GET FREE CONSUMER PROTECTION.

Use your credit card to make certain purchases—like airline tickets, car repairs and mail-order purchases—and get free protection from consumer ripoffs and good old-fashioned dissatisfaction. Under the Fair Credit Billing Act, you can refuse to pay the amount of the purchase and the finance charges, too, as long as you've attempted to work out disputes with the seller. Document everything. Phone calls don't prove anything.

154 DITCH THE MINIMUM INVESTMENT ON A MUTUAL FUND.

Some great mutual funds have minimum initial investment requirements that can be daunting to the small investor. Skip that by setting up an automatic investment plan, having $50 or so debited from your account monthly. Here are some funds that allow you to do so:

INVESCO EasiVest Plan 800-525-8085

Twentieth Century 800-345-2021

T. Rowe Price Automatic Asset Builder Plan (minimum of $100 a month) 800-638-5660.

Even if the mutual fund of your choice doesn't have a formal automatic investment plan advertised, ask if it will waive the minimum if you agree to one.

155 STOP PAYING HIGH CUSTODIAL FEES FOR IRAs.

Pay attention to what you are shelling out for parking your individual retirement account (IRA). Shop around among the different fund families and discount brokers for special deals. Janus will even allow you to pay a one-time fee of $100 that totally covers any IRAs you have and any you might add. And that fee is tax deductible.

156 PAY PEANUTS FOR COMMISSIONS.

If you absolutely want someone merely to execute your already well-thought-out trades, a deep discounter may be the way for you to go. These outfits charge roughly one-fifth of what you'd pay through a full-service brokerage. If you trade frequently, push for even deeper discounts than you are initially offered. Here are some of the more established ones:

K. Aufhauser 800-368-3668

Bidwell & Co. 800-547-6337

Brown Co. 800-225-6707

Pacific Brokerage Services 800-421-8395

Security Brokerage Services 800-421-8395.

If you want to know everything there is to know about discounter pricing, consult Mercer Inc.'s extensive survey. Call 800-582-9854 or 212-334-6212.

157 FREE HELP IN SAVING FOR YOUR CHILD'S COLLEGE.

You can also tap T. Rowe Price for a free College Planning Kit, filled with good information. It contains a step-by-step worksheet that lets you calculate exactly how much to invest each month to cover college expenses. Call 24 hours at 800-541-8467.

If you subscribe to Ben Franklin's "A penny saved is a penny earned" theory, perhaps you'd like The Franklin College Costs Planner. Call 800-342-FUND ext. 1442. Another fund offering a free copy is Founders' College Planning Guide at 800-525-2440.

If Fidelity has your number, get its free Fidelity College Savings Plan Fact Kit by dialing 800-544-8888.

Another good performer for college bound kids has been the Janus Funds. Call 800-525-8983 ext. 264 and ask about the Janus No Minimum Initial Investment Program. You can sign on for as little as $50 a month with no-load up front.

Another savings plan comes from Dreyfus Third Century Fund, which waives the typical $2,500 minimum investment and allows you to put in as little as $100 a month. Call 800-373-9387 and ask for information about The Dreyfus Step Program.

158 Free Forecasts of College Costs.

Several investment firms will estimate costs for a specific year and institution in the future. Contact:
The College Savings Bank (800-888-2723) will send you a planning package with worksheets.
The INVESCO Funds Group (800-525-8085), based in Denver, Colo., tracks costs at more than 3,000 colleges and universities. *T. Rowe Price* (800-638-5660) projects college costs and the amount you need to save to meet them.

159 Free Help in Applying to College.

Filling out multiple applications for colleges can be a pain. Call Collegelink at 800-944-8180 to find out about its painless program for mailing out applications with just one simple computer disk. You answer questions on a computer disk that they send you. Then the company formats your application for up to eight different schools (costs $5 per application).

160 Save Time and Money by Walking Through Campuses on Video.

Some services now specialize in campus tours for potential students, meaning you don't have to take expensive trips to visit some college or university you could have easily eliminated.

Detailed video tours of 300 schools are available for $15 apiece + shipping and handling from Collegiate Choice Walking Tours (201-871-0098).

161 LOW-COST COMPUTER GUIDES TO COLLEGE SCHOLARSHIP MONEY.

Besides buying a house, college is usually one of the largest expenditures. However, there is a mind-boggling array of scholarships available for those willing to do a little digging. For example, one small college in Pennsylvania found enrollment declining, so it began offering scholarships to students who lived at home and commuted to classes. Many of the scholarships are quirky. These services help you navigate the maze:

Available at 500 schools and public libraries is the College Cost Explorer: Fund Finder, an MS-DOS computer software program from The College Board (212-713-8165) that has details on more than 3,000 sources of financial aid. National College Services, Ltd. (800-662-6275) tracks more than 200,000 student aid programs and costs $30. Or if your high school guidance office, local library or college subscribes, a search will be free. The National Scholarship Research Service, Santa Rosa, Calif. 800-432-3782 will send you a free brochure and an application to fill out that aids its search for a match for you. The cost is $75. The company also produces a book called the Guide to Winning Scholarships ($20).

162 FREE INFORMATION ON SCHOLARSHIPS.

The National Scholarship Research Service is a clearinghouse for several scholarships and will send a free brochure and application to you if you call 707-546-6777. The U.S. Department of Education has prepared a booklet on paying for college. For a free copy of Preparing Your Child for College: A Resource

Book for Parents, call 800-872-5327. For a guide to federal sources of financial aid, call the Student Aid Hotline at the U.S. Department of Education (800-433-3243). Another key resource is your state's student finance commission, which can alert you to free seminars on the topic of getting funds for education. Incidentally, Orville Redenbacher Second Start Scholarships of $1,000 apiece are awarded each year to 25 back-to-schoolers over 30. For an application, write: P.O. Box 39101, Chicago, Ill. 60639.

You could also buy Winning Scholarships for College: An Insider's Guide by Marianne Ragins (published by Henry Holt). Ragins raked in more than $400,000 in scholarship offers and, in this book, she tells how to follow her plan. Ragins is now a graduating senior from Florida A&M University. She did not spend a penny of her own to get through school. The $120,000 she received in scholarships covered everything, including spending money.

163 INSTILL AN ENTREPRENEURIAL SPIRIT IN YOUR CHILD FOR FREE.

In recent years a cottage industry of expensive camps and seminars purporting to teach kids about business ownership has sprung up. One of the best programs around continues to be Junior Achievement (717-540-8000), and you don't pay an arm and a leg for your child (kindergarten through 12th grade) to join.

164 ASK FOR STUDENT DISCOUNTS ON EVERYTHING.

If you are a student anywhere—even for just a non-credit class in continuing education—flash your student ID card and get a surprising array of discounts. Student ID cards can get you discounts on everything from entertainment to equipment and supplies. Additionally, you'll have access to free lectures and movies on campus, as well as the college library. School libraries often have an amazing collection of useful material that your public library may not have.

165 FREE TRIAL OF DOW JONES TELERATE.

Get a sampling of electronically delivered market prices, economic news and analysis that financial decision makers worldwide rely upon. Call 800-472-3859.

166 CUT OUT INSURANCE COMMISSIONS.

If you are paying commissions to an insurance agent, you can save 10% or more off the cost of your insurance by purchasing insurance from a company that doesn't use agents. USAA (800-531-8000) cuts out the middleperson.

167 FREE TAX GUIDE ON COMMODITY FUTURES AND OPTIONS.

Call Amerivest Brokerage Services at 800-900-8000.

168 FREE GUIDE TO UNDERSTANDING REMICS AND MORTGAGE-BACKED SECURITIES.

Fannie Mae, the leading issuer of REMICS, has put together a free guide to understanding the risk and reward potential of this investment. Call 800-BEST-MBS or in Washington, D.C., call 202-752-6547.

169 FREE ADVICE ON THE BASICS OF INVESTING IN INTERNATIONAL STOCKS.

Call T. Rowe Price (800-541-4713; T. Rowe Price Investment Services, Inc., 100 East Pratt St., Baltimore, Md. 21202) and ask for the free report, The Basics of International Stock Investing.

170 FREE CREDIT CARDS.

Don't pay $25-100 for the right to have a credit card. There are plenty of cards around with no annual fees. And, for good customers, your credit card issuer will often drop the charge if you call the 800-number to politely request it. You can also get the interest rate dropped the same way. The customer service representative may initially balk, but this tactic almost always works, because competition for your credit card business is so stiff these days.

171 GET A FREE CREDIT REPORT.

Request a credit report once a year from each of the three major credit bureaus to mistake-proof your credit history. Here's how to get the reports. TRW gives you one free a year. The other two bureaus charge $8. Write the following companies and include a copy of a recent bill with your current address and your Social Security number, along with your request: Equifax Information Service, P.O. Box 105873, Atlanta, Ga. 30348, 404-612-2500, fax 404-612-3150 or 800-685-1111; TRW Complimentary Report Request, P.O. Box 2350, Chatsworth, Calif. 91313-2350 or 800-682-7654 and Trans Union, P.O. Box 7000, North Olmstead, Ohio 44070.

You are entitled to a free report any time you are turned down for credit. Get reports from all three companies, though, because consumers often find conflicting reports, and the credit bureaus have also been known to share erroneous information with each other. Mistakes are still common, and they are not easy to remove from your record. Yet with everyone from employers to loan officers taking a peek, taking the time to scan your report could pay off big.

172 NO ANNUAL FEES ON IRAS.

Maintaining an individual retirement account account may cost you $50 to $100 a year even if you make no changes to your investment. That's just for the privilege of parking your funds at a bank or brokerage house. Look for fee-free accounts, such as the one offered by Scudder, Stevens & Clark Inc. (Call 800-225-2470 ext. 8245 for a free copy of Scudder's No Fee IRA Handbook.)

173 GET FREE PROFESSIONAL ADVICE.

Don't hesitate to call a professional for advice because you assume the meter starts ticking immediately. Lawyers, accountants, financial planners, realtors and other professionals will typically provide an hour-long consultation for free in the hope of gaining your business. Here are phone numbers for the American Medical Association, 1101 Vermont Ave. N.W., 12th Floor, Washington, D.C. 2000 (202-789-7400); American Bar Association, 750 North Lake Shore Dr., Chicago, Ill. 60611 (312-988-5000) and the National Association of Realtors, 700 11th St. N.W., Washington, D.C. 20001-4507 (202-383-1000).

To get the most out of the session, know what you want to accomplish and take pertinent documents with you.

And remember, if you have been harmed by botched surgery or injured on the job, for instance, a law firm that believes in your claim will take on your case in return for a percentage of the hoped-for settlement.

Some doctors are also good about fielding phone calls at no charge, too. Ask about your doctor's policy.

174 GET HELP WITH COLLECTING CHILD SUPPORT.

Each year more than $4 billion goes unpaid in child support. Get your just due by contacting the Child Support Collection Association (800-729-2445). You pay only a $25 application fee. The company takes a 25% bounty on whatever it collects, but parents often find state agencies of little use.

175 Cheap Advice for Divorced Families.

Get a free referral list of experienced mediators in your area from the Academy of Family Mediators, 1500 S. Highway 100, Suite 355, Golden Valley, Minn. 55416; 612-525-8670 or 800-292-4AFM.

176 Do-It-Yourself Wills.

You can get software for writing a will for about $20. Just check to see if it is valid in your state to write one in such a manner. Hiring a lawyer to do a will costs $500 and up. However, if your estate is valued at more than $600,000, skip this advice.

177 Make Crime Pay...if You've Been a Victim.

Your state likely has a fund to compensate for expenses such as medical costs if you've been victimized by a crime. You could be eligible for $2,000 or more. However, few people are aware of these funds, which thus go untapped. Contact your local police department or the Office for Victims of Crimes (202-307-5983).

178 Making a Killing on Old Newspapers.

If you have an old newspaper that you think might be valuable, call the Serial And Government Publications division of the Library of Congress (202-707-5690) for a free memo on valuable old newspapers. Some dating from the late 1700s may fetch up to $10,000.

179 Information on Coins as Collectibles.

You can get good information on coins and their value from Benham Certified Metals (800-447-4653) and the Silver and Gold Report (800-289-9222; P.O. Box 109665, Palm Beach Gardens, Fla. 33410).

180 FREE LAW-SCHOOL TAX CLINICS.

If an envelope from the Internal Revenue Service gives you chills, you can get free help getting yourself out of a muddle with the agency. About 20 law schools nationwide are sponsoring free tax clinics where students give real clients advice on untangling messes wih the IRS and with state tax agencies. Here are some of the schools to contact:

American University, Washington, D.C.

Georgia State University, Atlanta

Illinois Institute of Technology, Chicago

Loyola University in Chicago and in New Orleans

Quinnipiac College, Bridgeport, Conn.

Rutgers University, Newark, N.J.

Southern Illinois University, Carbondale

Southern Methodist University, Dallas

University of California, Davis

University of Denver

University of Minnesota, Minneapolis

University of Nebraska, Lincoln

University of New Mexico, Albuquerque

Villanova University, Villanova, Pa.

Yeshiva University, New York.

If none of these schools is near you, and you've got a legal dispute regarding taxes, contact a law school in your area to see if it has recently initiated such a program. If you are headed for an audit and can't afford accounting help, contact accounting schools to see if they have free clinics.

Another route: The IRS Problem Resolution Program. If your tax problems have caused you a significant problem, you may qualify for free government help: Call 800-829-1040 and say you want to apply for a Taxpayer Assistance Order. You'll be sent Form 911, which will then be routed to the appropriate PRP.

181 FREE ADVICE ON SPRUCING UP YOUR HOME TO SELL.

You can boost your home's price by taking a few extra steps like repairing the caulking in bathrooms and cleaning the exterior of your water heater. Get a booklet of handy tips by calling the National Association of Realtors at 202-383-1000.

182 GREAT TIPS FROM EXPERTS ON HOW TO SAVE.

The Consumer Literacy consortium, an association of 23 consumer groups, has published a dynamite pamphlet called 66 Ways to Save Money, covering everything from car sales to checking accounts to life insurance. To get your copy, send a check for 50 cents to the Superintendent of Documents, "Save Money," Pueblo, Colo. 81009.

183 SAVE BIG BUCKS BY NEGOTIATING.

From Marc Eisenson, author of The Pocket Change Investor, come these tips on negotiating on almost everything: First, you have to ask. Determine what you would pay for the item and then give a low-ball offer.

Comparison shop and then snitch. Let the shopowner know what the competitor is offering and ask if he or she will beat the price. Know when to walk away.

Play let's make a deal if you are making more than one purchase.

Here are some dont's from Eisenson:

Don't reveal your bottom line.

It's no bargain if you put it on your credit card and
don't pay off the bill by the due date.

Don't buy new if you can possibly avoid it.

Don't shop when you're in a bad mood or on an
empty stomach.

Don't dicker if it's already a fair price.

184 PENNY-PINCHING A HOME CLOSING.

Buying a house is one of the biggest purchases you'll make in your lifetime. Why not slash costs while you can? First, get a copy of The Banker's Secret by Marc Eisenson (Villard Books, $14.95, which you can order by calling 914-758-1400). Some of his tips:

Strong ARM your way out of PMI (private mortgage insurance). Scrape together enough for a 20% downpayment, even if it means borrowing from relatives and getting an ARM (adjustable rate mortgage) loan. Otherwise, you'll have to pay mortgage insurance.

Talk with your tax preparer before setting a date for the closing. A few days can make a big difference on your tax deduction.

Get a last-minute check-up. Schedule another inspection of the home as close as possible to closing time. Get reimbursed by the seller at closing for any problems.

Chapter Three

CUSTOMER'S ALWAYS RIGHT

*Find everything from free professional haircuts to free
health club memberships and even get paid for your opinion.*

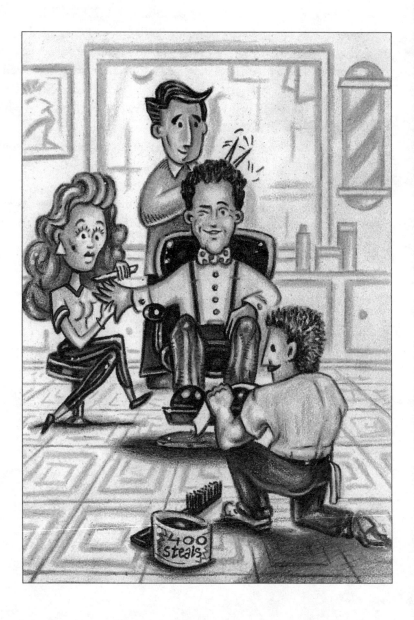

185 DISTRESS SALES.

Watch your local newspapers and strip malls for going-out-of-business and bankruptcy sales. Often, these stores just want to get rid of products simply to keep from having to pay carting costs. Wait until a day or two before the final closing to get absolute rock-bottom prices. For example, at a recent closeout of a shoestore in Atlanta, one consumer purchased three pairs of children's shoes for $11 total—essentially getting two pairs for free.

186 FREE HAIR STYLING.

Hair salons throughout the country will give you a haircut and/or color for free if you agree to serve as a model. Call and ask about the model night (also called class or training night). Don't worry about your tresses being decimated by some whacked-out wannabe: Apprentice stylists and colorists do the work while supervised by the pros. Top salons like Doyle Wilson in Los Angeles (213-658-6987), Scott Cole in Atlanta (404-237-4970), Geneses in Boston (617-236-4242) and Minardi Minardi in New York City (212-308-1711) all have these classes. If you are flexible, you'll come away with a whole new look that would have cost you $60-250 depending on what you had done.

187 FREE WEIGHTS—AND THE CLUBS THAT GO WITH THEM.

Wanna work out for free instead of shelling out hundreds of dollars for a health club membership? Cut a deal with the club manager. Look around for something you can do. Watch kiddies for a couple of hours a week in the club's nursery. Clean the weight machines. Offer your services as a trainer for a few hours a week. Or if you're in top form, teach a class or two in exchange for a membership. This strategy works virtually everywhere—from the local YMCA to the most chi-chi club in town. However, the management understandably likes to keep this fact quiet, so be prepared to give them the same hard sell they employ peddling their pricey memberships.

At the very least, push for a free month while you shop for clubs. Competition is so stiff in metropolitan markets that managers will approve your request if you stand firm in the face of their high-pressure sales tactics. You can also push for deep discounts if you agree to come in at a time of the day when the club isn't crowded.

Finally, when you do sign on, ask the manager to throw in extras like 10 hours of free babysitting, a free massage, a fistful of free guest passes and whatever else you can think of.

188 GET FREEBIES FOR YOUR OPINION.

Don't hang up on market researchers. You could literally be slamming the receiver down on $100 or more in cash or products. Companies are so desperate to know what's going on in your head that they are willing to pay a price to interrupt your dinner. The problem is, you won't know that unless you listen to the spiel. For instance, one consumer who answered a few questions about phone service, was subsequently paid $200 and received two months' worth of free long distance service for participating in testing a new service.

Market research companies are always looking for candidates for focus groups as well. Call market researchers and let them know you'd be available. You'll typically get $50 for an hour of your time, plus free products.

At the mall, stop and answer the questions, too. Again, for your civility and trouble, you get rewards like a free piece of luggage or free cellular phone, depending on the study.

Fields that are particularly ripe for such giveaways are computer software and communications firms, because they are so competitive. Fill out survey cards if you're a heavy user of computers. Microsoft, for instance, solicits advice from a network of good customers and, in return, ships them free software.

189 IF YOU ARE OF A CERTAIN AGE, TAKE ADVANTAGE OF IT.

Join the American Association for Retired Persons for $8 and gain access to thousands of dollars worth of discounts. Best of all, spouses of those age 55 and older are eligible no matter what their age. Just another advantage to that May-December marriage. Banks sometimes give free checking if you're over 50. Discounts on travel, entertainment and more abound. Some stores even have special days when seniors are given special discounts or double coupons.

190 FREE COPIES OF MAGAZINES AND NEWSLETTERS.

Don't subscribe before you're sure you really can use the information promised. Instead, always ask for a free sample copy of the publication and always accept offers on an issue or more for free. Then if you don't like it, just write canceled across the bill. Better yet, go to the library if you can afford the time out of the office.

191 FREE CLASSES AND MORE.

If you are considering taking a course, ask for one free lesson before you sign up. Karate classes, swimming lessons, darkroom courses, potterymaking—you name it and ask the instructor for a freebie. New Horizons Computer Learning Centers (714-556-1220), a nationwide computer training company, gives an introductory class worth $120 for free, hoping you'll return for more training. The Little Gym (800-352-4588), a children's exercise class, routinely gives coupons for one free session ($12 value), sometimes with a free water bottle or frisbee. Home Depot sponsors weekly clinics on a wide variety of topics for do-it-yourselfers. Recent offerings included how to install a ceiling fan, how to weatherize a deck and how to lay tile.

Similarly, retailers are allowing customers to sample the goods before you pay. For example, at most music stores you can now hear entire compact discs at listening booths, saving you from paying for a CD that might have been disappointing. Several athletic stores have sections where you can try that pair of Rollerblades or shoot a few hoops wearing the latest basketball shoes.

192 TAKE ADVANTAGE OF COMPANY COUPLINGS.

Be on the lookout for tie-ins that give you unexpected freebies. For example, Goodyear (800-GOODYEAR) recently teamed up with Holiday Inn to offer a second night free on a hotel stay for redeeming coupons that gave 10% off oil, lube and filter at a local service center.

193 CONTACT LOCAL MANUFACTURERS AND ASK IF THEY USE TESTERS.

You can often get some incredible deals just by making people aware of your existence. For example, Oshkosh B'Gosh, a manufacturer of children's clothing, tests kids clothes on tykes, then gives families coupons redeemable for free outfits. Shoe manufacturers often use testers. Toy companies want to know what your child thinks of their creations. Let your imagination run wild.

194 TIRED OF PAYING TOP-DOLLAR FOR UNDIES?

No more with D&A Merchandise Company (22 Orchard St., New York, N.Y. 10002; 212-925-4766). Get both men's and women's undergarments for 25-35% off retail. Send $2 for a catalog.

195 GET 50% AND MORE OFF DESIGNER CLOTHES AT OFF-PRICE STORES.

One word of caution to the new initiate to these wildly prolif-erating stores: Many of the items are irregulars (slight flaws) and seconds (more serious flaws). Check carefully to make sure you can live with the problem before you buy. Here are some of the best stores, with phone numbers to get locations nearest you:

Bolton's (201-941-9601). Women's clothing only.

Filene's Basement (800-666-4045). Stores in Massachu-setts, Minnesota, Illinois, New York, Washington, D.C., Pennsylvania, Connecticut, New Hampshire, Maine and Rhode Island. Flagship store with legendary bargains in men's and women's clothing in Boston.

Loehmann's (718-409-2000). More than 80 stores nationwide, this store was the originator of the concept. Women's clothes only. Best finds in sizes 4 and 6. Selections tend to be more upscale and thus pricier.

Marshalls (800-MARSHAL). Designers like Calvin Klein, Perry Ellis, Armani and Anne Klein. Offers men's, women's and children's clothing.

T.J. Maxx (800-926-6299). A hipper version of Marshalls, offering men's, women's and children's clothing.

Another good bet: the department store clearance centers that are popping up with increasing frequency in the outer reaches of the suburbs. Macy's, Neiman Marcus, Nordstrom, Rich's, Saks Fifth Avenue and other name stores slough off their unsold garments here. The quality is great and mark-downs are even better.

196 Name Brand Kid's Clothes at Factory Outlet Prices.

Olsen Mill Direct (800-537-4979) sells name brand children's clothes at deep discounts. Ask for a free catalog. You can also try "gently owned" children's clothing stores like The Children's Orchard. The stores demand that clothes be in almost new condition, cleaned and pressed—yet you pay one-fifth to one-third of the original cost.

197 Quality Men's Shirts at 50% Off.

Paul Frederick Shirt Company (223 West Poplar St., Fleetwood, Penn. 19522; 610-944-0909 or 800-247-1417) manufactures many of the private-label men's shirts you find in better stores. However, you can get the same shirts at 50% off retail prices by buying directly from the company through a free catalog.

198 Get 50% Off Diamonds (Without Making a Trip to 47th St. in Manhattan).

Get a 10-day free inspection on a GIA (Gemological Institute of America) certified diamond (from $1,000 to $1 million) at half the price you'd normally pay. Call Empire Diamond (800-SAVE-HALF, The Empire State Building, 66th floor, New York, N.Y.) and the company will fax or mail the documentation, and you get a 60-day money-back guarantee.

199 Get Great Buys on Photo Gear and Film Processing by Mail.

Here are some companies that offer good deals on camera gear and film:

KEH *Photo*, 800-DIAL KEH, 404-892-5522 or fax 404-897-2966, 188 14th St., N.W., Atlanta, Ga. 30318. It also purchases used equipment.

Mystic Color Labs 800-367-6061. Call for prices and free film mailers.

Porter's Camera Store, 319-266-0303, Box 628, Cedar Falls, Iowa 50613. Free catalogs with a range of heavily discounted photographic equipment and another with video accessories. Specializes in buying closeout equipment.

200 GIVE SECONDHAND SHOPS A SECOND CHANCE.

You are behind the times if thinking of thrift shops brings to mind dusty, dimly lit places with barely salvageable merchandise. These days you can get top quality sporting goods equipment at a franchise chain called Play It Again Sports. Get great music for one-fourth the original cost at Back Tracks. For a few hundred dollars or less, women can rent evening gowns, bridal gowns and bridesmaid dresses valued at thousands of dollars from shops with names like One Night Stand. You can skip garage sales but still get incredible bargains by shopping places like these. You'll see plenty of Lexuses, Mercedes-Benzes and BMWs in the parking lots. Getting great deals is chic.

201 GET FREE COMPUTER DISKS AND VHS TAPES.

Answer ads offering to send you free information on disks or on VHS tapes. Computer magazines often carry such ads. Retirement homes and colleges routinely send out videos with their ads. After you've looked at the information, simply reformat the disk or record over the tapes for your own use.

202 GET MAKEUP AND PERFUME AT 90% OFF RETAIL PRICES.

The cosmetics industry has long been noted for its huge markups. Get name brands like Estee Lauder, Oscar de la

Renta, Giorgio, Maybelline, Cutex and more from Beauty Boutique, 6836 Engle Road, Cleveland, Ohio 44130 or 216-826-1712. You can order a free catalog.

203 VALUABLE INFORMATION FOR FREE FROM THE RETAILERS YOU LOVE.

Retailers are falling all over themselves to get you to come into their stores. Part of the come-on has sparked a consumer education revolution. Stores want to buy your good will by giving you all sorts of money-saving tips. Before you dismiss the free videos, informational booklets, seminars and toll-free hotlines as self-serving claptrap designed to separate you from your hard-earned greenbacks, investigate them. But you must get into the habit of asking for them because they aren't always well advertised.

For example, several stores now sponsor free classes on useful topics. Home Depot (404-433-8211) sponsors twice-weekly clinics in its stores for do-it-yourselfers, depending on what's popular in the region. Recent offerings included woodworking, water heater installation, installing a security system and building a deck or fence. Home Depot also has an in-store computer on which you can produce a free, 3-D remodeling plan for your kitchen or other rooms in your house.

Blockbuster Video stores—about 4,000 in the U.S.—have a small corner of their gigantic superstores reserved for free rental videos, primarily how-tos on topics like teaching your kids about safety, childproofing your house and more. Members present their cards to check them out.

204 HIRE A PERSONAL SHOPPER FOR FREE.

You don't have to be a big spender to qualify for shopping services available at most department stores. Most consumers still don't realize that personal shoppers don't charge for the service.

You also don't have to be planning a large purchase. If time is money, having someone else do the legwork can mean savings. You can even instruct the personal shopper to head to the discount racks. Call ahead and explain what you're seeking. The shopper, who is paid by the store, will then typically meet you with three or four items in your price range.

205 OUTLET MANIA FOR 25-75% OFF NAME BRANDS.

In the last several years, shopping at outlet malls has gradually lost its downscale air and has now become a major factor in the economy. Indeed, department stores are hurting and that's largely due to the appeal of outlets. Believe it or not, there is even an annual magazine that tracks outlets called The Joy of Outlet Shopping (15950 Bay Vista Drive, Suite 250, Clearwater, Fla. 34620; 813-536-4047 or 800-669-1020; $5), which is a good guide to the nation's 20,000 outlet stores and 750 outlet centers. This handy magazine carries $200 in outlet coupons.

To get even better buys at outlets, call and ask about special sales days. Often all the merchants at a mall will designate a particular special promotion near the holidays. One of the nation's best is Warehouse Row (615-267-1111) in Chattanooga, Tenn. Boasting 50 stores such as Bass, Polo, Ruff Hewn and Perry Ellis, this mall is in a beautifully renovated warehouse in downtown.

206 DESIGNER CLOTHES AT 75% OFF.

If dressing well is the best revenge, take time when you're in New York City on business or pleasure to visit your favorite designer's showroom. In the garment district, sample sales are rampant, and you can pick up incredible buys on clothing you normally couldn't touch. Giorgio Armani, Adrienne Vittadini, Alexander Julian, Polo—you name them, the sales are happening. The catch? Most items are in model sizes, meaning a size 6 or 8 for women and a size 40R jacket for men. Women's shoes are size 6; men's size 10. If you can't fit those sizes, you can pick up some impressive gifts for a little moulah.

The Bargain Hotline (212-540-0123) is updated weekly on Friday nights and lists upcoming sample and overstock sales in garment center showrooms. This terrific hotline also lets you know the addresses, payment accepted and the types of merchandise available. You can only call from a phone within the New York area and the call costs $1.95 for the first minute and 75 cents a minute after that.

If you visit New York frequently, consider a subscription to the S&B Report (Lazar Media Group, 108 East 38 St., New York, N.Y. 10016, 212-683-7612; $49 annually for a newsletter with 50-300 different sample sales listed each month).

Another option: Call your favorite designer directly and ask to be put on the mailing list for sample sales.

207 GET A REPLACEMENT FOR FREE.

If you have a special pair of cowboy boots or some other beloved item, sometimes approaching the manufacturer even past the warranty date can yield unexpectedly wonderful results. One woman knew her husband was really bummed when his favorite pair of Justin Boots developed a crack in the leather. Although they were admittedly well-worn and well-traveled, she sent them to the manufacturer in hope it would repair the problem. Justin Boots went the extra mile and sent a brand new pair of the same boots.

A Motorola dealer replaced one of the company's popular flip-phones—despite the fact that it was three years old and had been chewed by its owner's dog.

Likewise, if you've lost a small part of a product, don't junk it. Write the manufacturer first: You'll often get a replacement part free of charge. For a catalog for replacement parts for

Fisher Price Toys, write Consumer Affairs, 636 Girard Ave., E. Aurora, N.Y. 14052-1880.

208 RETURNING DEFECTIVE MERCHANDISE WITHOUT THE HASSLE.

Think you're stuck if that new steam-iron breaks and you don't have the receipt? Think again. Buy the exact same model, saving the box and receipts, then return the defective item to the store whence it came in the first place. You don't have to be stuck with their mistakes.

Companies like Victoria's Secret and Parisians have liberal return policies. Managers often have wide discretion when it comes to the traditional 30-day returns. Always maintain your cool, but firmly inform the store management what would satisfy your complaint.

209 GRAZE WHILE YOU SHOP.

Saturday is typically the day when grocery stores have tantalizing samples free for the nibbling. A recent trip through a grocery store yielded a cup of gourmet coffee, spicy shrimp, grapefruit and sauteed shiitake mushrooms. Don't be shy.

210 GET THE FREEBIES COMING TO YOU FROM YOUR CREDIT CARD MERCHANT.

Because department stores have been losing so much charge card business to Visa, MasterCard, American Express and Discover, several have recently introduced nifty freebies for their best charge card customers. If you have a department store credit card and spend a minimal amount, you can be upgraded to special programs that reward you with free gift wrap, alterations and delivery, as well as newsletters tipping you off to special sales. Macy's Presidents Club (800-341-7502) and Bloomingdale's Premier Gold

(212-705-2000) have the best benefits. Sears and Penney's also have good programs. The only card that turns out not to be such a great deal is Neiman Marcus' NM Plus, which has a $50 annual fee. What does make sense if Neiman Marcus is a favorite store is to spend enough—paying your bills monthly, of course—to rack up the $3,000 in charges to qualify for Neiman Marcus' InCircle (800-NCIRCLE). Those shoppers get special product samples, special sales days in the stores, travel at a discount and complimentary gift wrap. Meanwhile, at Nordstrom (800-964-1800), all shoppers are apparently created equally, and they are automatically feted with free gift wrapping, gift boxes and shipping with no annual fee for the Nordstom store card.

211 CELEBRATE THE MOMENTS OF YOUR LIFE ON OTHERS' TABS.

Don't be shy when retailers ask for your birthday. You could be in for some great gifts. For example, Wolf Camera (404-633-9000), an Atlanta-based photo chain, sends as a present to customers a coupon for a free picture frame or free film development. Takeout Taxi, a restaurant delivery chain, sends coupons for a free dinner to the restaurant from which you order the most. Baskin-Robbins sends coupons for a free double dip. Several restaurants have started birthday programs that entitle you to a free meal on your birthday. All you have to do is show a photo ID with your birthdate for proof.

If you are celebrating an anniversary or honeymooning, be sure to let hotels and restaurants know. Hotels and resorts will often treat you to a free overnight stay on your anniversary if you honeymooned there. Call well in advance and ask for the public relations manager or concierge and explain how special this trip is. Or if you decide to go at the last minute, be bold and let everyone at the hotel know this occasion is special and why. Being a blabbermouth will net you a room upgrade and sometimes niceties like a free bottle of wine, flowers and hors d'oeuvres.

212 GET FREE GIFTS FOR YOUR BABY (AND NOT JUST FROM YOUR RELATIVES AND FRIENDS).

New baby? Call the toll-free numbers often listed on the packages of the baby items you use and spread the good news. Manufacturers will shower you with coupons and free products. One young mom got $200 worth of products from eight phone calls.

Coupons can be requested from the following:

Beechnut 800-523-6633

Carnation 800-782-7766 (Its Special Delivery Club includes a free planner for new parents, samples and coupons throughout the first year.)

Enfamil & Lactofree Formula 800-422-2902

Gerber 800-443-7237*

Heinz Baby Juice 800-872-2229 (You can request a free copy of the Infant Feeding Guide, which comes with free coupons.)

Pregestimil 800-222-9123

Similac, Isomil & Alimentum 800-BABYLINE (Call to join the Welcome Addition Club.)

*Gerber will send you two cases of free formula if you have multiple births and double the amount of coupons.

213 FREE REPAIRS ON SMALL APPLIANCES.

Save receipts, owner's manuals and warranties. Habitually file them together in a readily accessible place. With electronics and other small items, you'll often find repairs are free if you have proof of purchase. Repairs can be extremely costly, so keeping these materials can pay off handsomely. Radio Shack (800-THE-SHACK) is a good source of information and has a good return policy.

214 Don't Turn Up Your Nose at Generics.

The manufacturers of name-brand goods often produce the exact same item under store labels. The only question you should be asking yourself is whether you want to foot the bill for a well-advertised product's promotional campaign or if a nice no-name item will do, thank you very much.

215 Discounted Wine by Mail.

Topline Wine and Spirits sells a fine selection at discounted prices by mail. Call or write for a free catalog: 4718 San Fernando Road, Glendale, Calif. 91204; 818-500-9670. Gold Medal Wine Club (800-266-8888) has premium wines at a 45% discount off retail prices.

E.C. Kraus Home Winemaking Equipment and Supplies (P.O. Box 7850, Independence, Mo. 64054; 816-254-7448) carries plastic stoppers that will preserve a bottle of wine for a few extra days.

Additional ways to save on wine: Look for discounters in your Yellow Pages. Choose a favorite brand, buy by the case and ask the manager for a special discount.

216 Try Government Auctions for Big Purchases.

If you want to get incredible buys on everything from cars to real estate to restaurant equipment, check out the government's offerings. These goodies were gained through foreclosures, bankruptcies, seizures and other means.

217 Get Designer Kids Clothes at 85% Off.

Kid News ($24.95; P.O. Box 797, Forest Hills, N.Y. 11375; $24.95 a year) tells you where to buy great children's clothing at a mind-boggling 85% off. Kids Report (212-982-9300; $29) is handy if you live close enough to Manhattan to take advantage of showroom sales.

218 DISCOUNTS ON BARBEQUE EQUIPMENT BY MAIL.

You can get terrific items from top-of-the-line barbeque grills to seasonings through the mail from Barbeques Galore (15041 Bake Parkway, Irvine, Calif. 92718; 800-GRILL-UP), which has superstores primarily on the West Coast.

219 NEVER PAY FULL PRICE FOR DRY CLEANING.

Frequent shopping plans, prepaid programs and special promotions have become routine in the dry-cleaning business. Do lots of comparison shopping before you award your business to a cleaner. EcoMat/EcoClean (212-769-1777), an environmentally sound chain of cleaners based in New York, gives $20 worth of free dry cleaning in exchange for a $100 prepayment. Look for coupons that give you free cleaning on your birthday or 50% off.

220 NEW PRODUCT INFORMATION.

Manufacturers introducing new products may offer discount coupons or free samples. These will frequently be included in information kits advertised in magazines and newspapers. If it's something you might use, be sure to request information. A recent offer from Boston Envision Contact Lenses for a free information kit (800-895-3618) on lenses that allow more oxygen to get to your eyes, making them a possibility for people who'd been told they couldn't tolerate contacts, included discount coupons. Another example: A free information kit on the New Ford Explorer (800-214-2648) included a discount offer from a local dealer.

221 WINNING FREE GIFTS.

In general, those dinky contests that flood your mailbox are a ripoff. A tip-off to a scam is when the company asks you to pay a mailing and processing fee to receive your prize. However, there are some companies that routinely award free gifts to customers for ordering. One reputable company that does this is Michigan Bulb Company. For ordering, you are generally rewarded with anything from free film developing from the Mystic Color Lab (800-367-6061; value $6.75) to a grand prize of $100,000. Just be cautious about the offers to which you reply. Another common ripoff: Those letters that say you've definitely won a certain prize if you come to see a time-share. Numerous consumers have been disappointed with nearly worthless "gifts" for their trouble. First, it's time consuming and, second, these outfits virtually trap you in a room and try to make you buy whatever their selling. Don't waste your time no matter how tempting the "free" gift might sound.

222　FREE GIFTS WITH A PURCHASE.

Be on the lookout for good deals when it comes to extras you can get just for buying a certain product. Makeup companies are famous for rewarding customers with "gifts," often with a retail value of $50 or more. The catch is you have to buy a certain amount of their products to get the gift. Is it worth it? That depends. If you typically use the product anyway, waiting to time your purchase to get a bonus for your money makes sense. Companies are going to great lengths to get your attention, so let them. Publications also frequently sponsor giveaways to attract new subscribers. You might wait to subscribe until a bonus is attached. For example, Sports Illustrated sometimes runs promotions where you get a free video on the best hits in football or some other sport.

223　CHARGE AIRLINE TICKETS, CATALOG ORDERS AND OTHER BIG TICKET ITEMS TO MASTERCARD OR VISA.

Both of these cards offer broad, free protection to consumers who might otherwise be stuck if a company goes out of business or fails to deliver a product. If that happens to you, ask your credit card company to issue a chargeback, and you get a full refund from the credit issuer. If your issuer balks, contact MasterCard International (800-627-8372) directly. If you write a check or pay cash for these items, you have no recourse but to sue if you're not satisfied. Consumers are largely unaware that chargebacks can save them a bundle.

224 HELP COMPANIES CELEBRATE AND GET FREE GIFTS.

On special anniversaries, retailers celebrate by giving customers big breaks and sharing the wealth. Watch for such special announcements. You'll often get free gifts just for walking through the door. For a grand opening recently, Just Wallpaper, a chain, ran a contest with no purchase necessary for three rooms of free wallpaper.

On holidays, too, you may get a gift for walking through the door. On Mother's Day, for instance, a grocery chain gave the first 5,000 customers a choice of several plants as a present.

225 TAKE ADVANTAGE OF SAMPLING.

Food and cosmetics companies have long known the power of letting customers sample the wares. Others have recently caught on. Again, the little gifts that come in the mail as a result should motivate you to fill out response cards on new product surveys. Freebies magazine (805-566-1225 or fax 805-566-0305; P.O. Box 5025, Carpinteria, Calif. 93014; $8.95 for a year's subscription or $12.95 for two years) has listings for dozens of samples from national companies—everything from children's computer software to financial booklets—usually for the price of a stamp.

226 GOOD CUSTOMERS GET WHAT THEY ASK FOR.

When you make a big purchase, look around for something the retailer will gladly kick in to make sure you're happy. For instance, when you shell out a couple of thousand bucks for a new sofa, ask for the print and extra throw pillows that pulled your eye to the sofa in the first place. You may have to wait until the display is disassembled, but you've still gotten some great accessories for free.

227 SPEAK UP ABOUT YOUR LIKES AND DISLIKES.

Thanks to sophisticated computer tracking systems, frequent customers of places ranging from grocery stores to the Ritz-Carlton are having their preferences recorded. At the grocery store, this information can mean more free offers from manufacturers of products you buy frequently. At the Ritz, for example, if you like the London Daily News, The New York Times, USA Today and The Wall Street Journal, you can expect those papers delivered free of charge upon your second stay with the hotel.

228 ASK FOR BIG BREAKS IF YOU'RE A FREQUENT CUSTOMER.

If you stop in often at a restaurant, hotel or store, get to know the manager and ask for a discount every once in a while. Loyalty is a prized quality and just by asking you'll likely save yourself 10% or more. For instance, grocery store chains, hair salons and restaurants like Chili's (800-352-4289) have begun to offer frequent shopper cards.

229 FREE REWARDS FOR BEING A GOOD CUSTOMER.

Loyalty is a valuable commodity these days. Watch for special programs that reward you just for being a good customer. The catch is they aren't always incredibly obvious. For example, AT&T ran a promotion in March 1995 offering all its customers a free weekend's worth of long distance calls. However, you didn't automatically get your free calls. You had to dial a toll-free number and request them. So be alert and grab your benefits.

230 VITAMINS AT 20% OFF RETAIL.

For discounts on vitamins, call Nutrition Warehouse Inc. at 800-645-2929 or 516-741-2929.

231 BOOKS FOR FREE (OR DISCOUNTED).

Waldenbooks (800-322-2000 ext. 400 or 203-353-2000) has a preferred reader program. For a $10 annual fee, you get 10% off all purchases in the store. Every time you spend $100, you get a gift certificate for an additional $5 off your next purchase. Borders Books and Barnes & Noble also have 10-20% off most of their books.

You can get hardcover books at a fraction of their original cost at bookstores in outlet malls. These bookstores (Bookstar is one chain) specialize in buying publishers' overstocks. Hence, the price is typically about one-fourth the original cover price.

For college students with a specific major, joining a book club can be smart. Pre-register for classes and ask your professors for the reading list. Then order from a book club specializing in that topic. For instance, history majors could try The History Book Club, Camp Hill, Pa. 17012, 717-697-6443.

The catch with book clubs is that each month they send cards to members that require you to check a selection or tell them not to send their selected Book-of-the-Month. If you fail to mail in that card, you automatically get a book and are billed for it. And returning it is often impossible or difficult, not to mention costly and time consuming. Some of the best known are: The Book of the Month Club, The Quality Paperback Book Club, the Children's Book Club, Homestyle Book Club and Money Book Club. All can be reached at 717-697-6443. Generally, they offer a choice of four books for $1 plus shipping and handling.

Think very carefully before signing up for one of these clubs, because you can be tripped up and wind up wasting money.

Upper Access Books (P.O. Box 457, Hinesburg, Vt. 05461 or 800-356-9315) specializes in hard-to-find books. Some of the merchandise is heavily discounted because the books are slightly damaged—a scratch on the cover or whatever. Ask for a free catalog.

Used bookstores sometimes yield good buys, too. Look for a store that gives you credit on trade-ins. Face it, rarely do you read a book twice. Why not make it do double duty for you?

232 FREE CIRCUS TICKETS.

If you have a child born in 1993, the same year as a pair of baby elephants, send the child's name and birthdate with your name and address to: Ringling Brothers Barnum & Bailey Circus, P.O. Box 5265, Clifton, N.J. 07015. You'll get one free ticket for that child to attend the circus.

233 BUY GENERIC DRUGS AND SAVE 50%.

By law, generics must have the same potency as name brands. Let your doctor know you want a generic rather than the name brand. Otherwise, you may unwittingly help send a doctor on a free vacation to Jamaica as a reward from the drug manufacturers for brand name loyalty.

234 PUSH STORES TO HAVE A "WE WON'T BE UNDERSOLD" POLICY.

Some stores advertise such stances. But if you shop at a store that doesn't and later see something you bought at a competitor's for half the price, take it back to the retailer and ask for a reduction. You may get your request.

235 KEEP SAFE ON THE ROAD FOR FREE.

Car-X Muffler & Brake is offering free "Call Police" signs to those who write: Car-X Muffler & Brake, 8430 W. Bryn Mawr, Suite 400, Chicago, Ill. 60631-9033.

236 SHOP AT OFF-PEAK TIMES AND GET REWARDS.

To draw customers at times when business is traditionally slow, retailers sometimes will give free gifts. For example, on a Tuesday night, customers who rented three or more videos at Blockbuster were presented with a goody box containing free food samples from several manufacturers, as well as several coupons for food products.

237 JOIN A WAREHOUSE CLUB.

Typically you'll pay a $25 membership fee upfront to join a warehouse club (Price Club, Costco, Pace, Sam's Wholesale Club, Supersaver and others). Is it worth the initiation fee? First, make a visit as the guest of a friend who belongs, or look for coupons in your credit card flyers that give you a free membership. Or call and ask the club manager if he or she will waive the fee for one day to allow you to check out the store. Look over the merchandise to see if joining would make sense for you. These clubs have much more than groceries. They sell everything from tires to garden hoses to sheets. You can save 20% to 60% if you shop carefully, but the deals are often mixed in with items that you could purchase for less elsewhere. Have an idea of prices for comparison when you go in.

BJ's 800-257-2582 ($25 annually);

Price Club 800-597-7423 ($30 annual fee for businesses; $35 for individuals);

Sam's Club 800-925-6278 ($25 annually).

Sam's Club even has an Auto Buying Program (501-273-1333) where it teams up with local car dealers to give members great deals on new and used cars.

238 CUT YOUR GROCERY BILLS BY UP TO 50%.

If you hate clipping coupons but like the savings they bring, you can have the best of both worlds by signing on with the Coupon Connection of America (for information, send a SASE to: 670 Welford Road, Suwanee, Ga. 30174 or call 800-466-9222 ext. 2180.) You can buy its Coupon Connection of America Grocery Coupon Certificate Book for $24.95. The book contains 20 $10 coupon certificates that you can redeem and request coupons for the specific brands you buy. You can select from more than 1,200 national brand name products. That's a $200 value for a $24.95 investment. And if you use a store that doubles coupons, your savings are multiplied. The coupons are good at any store.

239 GET THE BEST DEAL ON A NEW CAR.

You need to know what the dealer's price is to give you some negotiating strength. Here are services that will give you that information:

Auto Advisor (3123 Fairview Ave. E., Seattle, Wash. 98102; 800-326-1976 or 206-323-1976 or fax 206-323-1995) specializes in scientific research on the automotive market and is a consumer's consulting and buyer's service founded in 1977. The company typically saves 15-25% for its customers who pay a flat fee of $335 to enlist Auto Advisor to find the best deal on a car within a certain distance from your home. It claims that more than 67% of its clients get cars below the dealer's invoice price. Auto Advisor also analyzes deals prior to final signature for a $67 fee. Recent deals include $1,750 below invoice on an Acura Legend and a Jeep Grand Cherokee at $600 below invoice. It even negotiates discounts on Saturns, despite the company's widely publicized no-deal position. Auto Advisor frequently works with clients with disabilities to whom manufacturers will give additional stipends.

Other Resources – *AAA Auto Pricing Service* (900-776-4222; $1.95 a minute; American Automobile Association, 1000 AAA Drive, Heathrow, Fla. 32746-5063; 407-444-8030).
Car Bargains (800-475-7283) for $135 tells you the dealer's cost, then it'll get five quotes from dealers in your area.
Nationwide Auto Brokers, Southfield, Mich. 800-521-7257 ($11.95 for the first quote; $9.95 for additional quotes).

If you want to shop for your car on-line, get on the World Wide Web and dial Car Connect at http://www.carconnect.com/ to peruse used-car ads complete with pictures, for free. On CompuServe, you can go to the AutoNet Showroom (Go NEWCAR) and for $1.50 per car you can find out what your dealer paid for the new car you're eyeing. You can also connect with AutoVantage (Go ATV), a service that gives you the going rate for new and used cars. (You can do a trial with the company for $1 for three months.) Surf the Internet and on the Car Newsgroup (rec.autos.marketplace) you can buy, sell and trade.

One caveat: If you do not buy your car in the state where you register it, you may lose your lemon law protection.

240 Free Expert Help if You've Been Scammed.

The National Fraud Information Center has a toll-free number for you if you suspect you've been had. Call 800-876-7060 weekdays from 8:30 a.m. to 5:30 p.m. Counselors will direct you to the appropriate authorities in your state.

241 Almost Free Advice on the Best Toys.

Overwhelmed by all the choices for children's toys, videos and books? Get the annual awards issue of Parents' Choice magazine, available in late November, in which experts, kids and parents rate more than 200 products. Send $3 to Parents' Choice, P.O. Box 185, Newton, Mass. 02168. You can also get one free issue of Children's Software Revue by calling 313-480-0040.

242 CUT 30% OFF YOUR GROCERY BILL.

Get advice on getting the most out of coupons by snagging a copy of Thrifty Times, P.O. Box 6164, Scottsdale, Ariz. 85261. Some general tips from editor Melanie Lee Johnston:

*Shop at stores that double coupons.

*Match your coupons to sale items in the store's circular.

*Only clip coupons for items you routinely buy or for those you'd try if the price was right.

243 BEST DEALS ON BOUQUETS.

If you like to send flowers for special occasions, skip your local florist and go right to the source, nixing the extra charges florists tack on just for taking your order. Best bets: 24-hour phone service with 1-800-THE-ROSE (which follows your first order with a $10 coupon off your next one) or 1-800-FLOWERS.

Another good choice is Calyx & Corolla, a San Francisco mail-order firm that ships directly from growers and therefore discounts. Call 800-800-7788 for a free catalog. One of the lowest-cost chains is American Wholesale Floral. If there is one in your town, check it out. Flowers there are typically one-third the cost you'd find elsewhere.

244 RENT INSTEAD OF BUYING SPECIAL ITEMS.

If you have a big job like tilling your garden or you want to go camping with your kids, consider renting your gear rather than buying it at 20 times or more the cost of a one-day rental. Another option: Talk to your neighbors about chipping in for one neighborhood leaf-blower, riding mower, extension ladder, etc. That way your garage isn't crammed with expensive items you rarely use.

Chapter Four

SHOCK THERAPY

*Health-care cost savings? Check out how to get free
specialty care or no-cost immunizations.*

245 FREE HOTLINES FOR YOUR HEALTH.

There are hundreds of hotlines for health-related issues. To order the Directory of National Helplines, which lists 500 handy hotlines, send $7 to Pierian Press, P.O. Box 1808, Ann Arbor, Mich. 48106. The book is also on-line at your local library. Meanwhile, here are some of the most heavily used:

Alcohol and Drug Helpline 800-821-4357

American Board of Medical Specialties 800-776-2378 (To confirm that a doctor is board certified in the specialty claimed.)

American Heart Association 800-AHA-USA1

Boys Town National Hotline 800-448-3000

CDC AIDS Hotline 800-342-2437

Cancer Information Service 800-4CANCER

Lung Line 800-222-5864

National Mental Health Association 800-969-6642

National Victim Center 800-FYI-CALL.

246 FREE HEALTH CARE.

You may qualify for free health care. Contact medical teaching facilities and ask about clinical trials, or send a postcard to the Clinical Center for the National Institutes of Health, Office of Communications, NIH Clinical Center, Building 10, Room 1C255, Bethesda, Md. 20892-1170; 301-496-2563. You'll get a free brochure explaining patient admission procedure. Currently, 1,000 NIH trials are ongoing. In some cases, your travel tab to and from treatment will be picked up as well if you fit the doctors' bill.

Testing new drugs is often done by private companies these days, too. Watch for ads in your local paper seeking volunteers for certain studies. For example, one company was doing a study on a new type of birth control and its impact on osteoporosis. If you met the qualities the company was looking for, you were eligible for a free examination every six months including free mammograms, pap smears and bone density tests, as well as free birth control for five years. If you participated in the study for the entire five year period, you also received $700 or more.

247 THE BEST DRUGS ARE FREE.

Don't reach for your wallet so quickly when your doctor prescribes a drug for what ails you. Ask for samples. Doctors' medicine chests often overflow with them, but they don't necessarily think to offer if you don't ask. An extra benefit: If the drug doesn't work, you haven't wasted money on it.

Another option: generic drugs. A 10-day supply of brand name penicillin costs $15-60, while generic versions run from $7-20. You can order prescription and generic drugs through the mail from several firms. For price quotes and information on how to order prescription drugs by mail, call Action Mail Order at 800-452-1976, P.O. Box 787, Waterville, Maine 04903; 207-873-6226. Ask for a catalog and get a $5 coupon for your first order.

You can also try the American Association of Retired Persons (AARP) at 800-456-2277; or for price comparisons call the AARP Pharmacy Quote Center at 800-456-2226; Family Pharmaceuticals, P.O. Box 1288, Mount Pleasant, S.C. 29465 or 800-922-3444 and Medi-Mail, 871-C Grier Drive, Las Vegas, Nev. 89119 or 800-331-1458.

To learn more about generics, send for Guide to Interchangeable Drugs, a free 32-page booklet from the Generic Pharmaceutical Industry Association, 200 Madison Ave., Suite 2404, New York, N.Y. 10016.

248 FREE ADVICE ON FOOD SAFETY.

Wondering how long to keep that chicken salad? Save yourself a bout with food poisoning. Get free advice on food safety from the Department of Agriculture's Meat and Poultry Hotline (800-535-4555).

249 Buy Contact Lenses and Glasses by Mail and Save.

When your eyes are involved, quality is important, but you can still have discounts, too. In fact, magazines and newspapers of late have had some offers of free samples of contact lenses. Take advantage of such deals and save as much as 50% off. Here are some mail-order discounters in eyewear. Get a doctor's written prescription and mail or fax it to the following:

Contact Lens Supply (800-833-7525)

Lens Connection (800-695-5367)

Lens Direct (free catalog; P.O. Box 147, Hewlett, N.Y. 11557; 800-772-5367)

Lens Express (800-666-5367)

Precision Optical (free catalog specializes in reading glasses; 815-562-2174; 507 Second Ave., Rochelle, Ill. 61068)

Sunglasses USA (free catalog, specializes in Ray Bans; 800-872-7297).

250 Choosing a Nursing Home.

Besides going to college, this choice will be one of the most expensive you make for loved ones or for yourself. Indeed, nursing homes typically cost about $35,000 a year and complicated rules determine Medicare coverage. Many older folks mistakenly think they are eligible, but you are allowed very few assets before you qualify. Get a consumer's guidebook that covers the admission process by contacting: American Association of Homes and Services for the Aging, 901 E St. N.W., Washington, D.C. 20004-2037 or 800-508-9442 or 202-783-2242. The agency also sells Nursing Homes and You: Partners in Care ($8.95 + $3.50 shipping and handling) for families of Alzheimer's sufferers.

251 FREE INFORMATION ON PREPARING LIVING WILLS.

A pamphlet called Advanced Medical Directives: What Americans Need to Know About Their Rights explains living wills and powers of attorney for health care. It is available free with a SASE (55 cents) by writing Life-Fax, P.O. Box 501136, Atlanta, Ga. 31150 or calling 404-552-4140.

252 WOMAN'S HEALTH DIARY.

To keep up with your examinations, mammograms and other health issues, order a free diary by calling the Breast Health Center at Hahnemann University in Philadelphia at 215-762-3627.

253 BUY DISABILITY INSURANCE DIRECT FROM THE INSURER.

Disability insurance has gotten cheaper in the last few years but is still pricey. Shop around and get quotes from at least five insurers. To save the agent's commission, check with the USAA Life Insurance Company (9800 Fredericksburg Road, San Antonio, Texas 78288; 800-531-8000 ext. 83322). It allows you to buy directly.

254 GET TOP NOTCH EXPERT CARE—FREE.

Especially if your case is slightly unusual, you might be surprised at the well-known doctors who will take time to give you plenty of free advice over the phone. Kim Brady, a 39-year-old Baltimore woman with an unusual heart problem and trouble with her high-tech pacemaker, tracked down the inventor of the pacemaker who agreed to provide her a readjustment for no charge. Brady was surprised at how many nationally known specialists would spend hours discussing her case on the phone.

255 GET SPECIALTY CARE FREE BY BEING A PRACTICE CASE.

Podiatry, dental and chiropractic schools often give free assessments and low-cost services to those willing to let students—supervised by pros, of course—hone their skills on them. Thus, getting a $600 root canal might cost you the price of materials alone—less than $150. You can have a cavity filled for $20-25, a 60% savings. Look in the Yellow Pages, and call the school offering the service you need and find out when students will be available.

256 FREE ADVICE ON YOUR DIET.

To get a detailed booklet that explains the appropriate food for your weight and activity level, contact the American Diabetes Association at 800-232-3472 or the American Dietetic Association at 312-899-0040. Ask for a free copy of Exchange Lists for Meal Planning, a 32-page guide packed with easily understandable information.

257 FREE CHILD IMMUNIZATIONS AND MORE.

Accidents are the number one killer of children, and there are low-cost precautions you can take that can literally be life-savers for your children. To get Accident Prevention: A Family Guide to Child Safety for free, send a self-addressed, business-size envelope to Accident Prevention, Room 176B, Baylor College of Medicine, One Baylor Plaza, Houston, Texas 77030 or call 713-798-4712.

For a free immunization schedule for babies, send a SASE to SHOTS, March of Dimes, 1275 Mamaroneck Ave., White Plains, N.Y. 10605. The phone number is 914-428-7100. Before age 2, children need 15 different inoculations, and in the U.S. an alarming 50% of all children are improperly immunized, making them vulnerable to easily preventable diseases. For a free pocket-sized immunization chart, send a business-sized SASE to Kids Chart (English version) or Spanish Chart (Spanish version), Healthtex, P.O. Box 21488, Greensboro, N.C. 27420-1488.

What most families don't realize is that vaccines are available free at your local health clinic, whereas you can easily spend $500 or more having your pediatrician vaccinate your child before he or she reaches school. At the clinic you may have to pay a small processing fee—usually under $10—for each visit, but it represents a large savings.

258 KEEP KIDS SAFE FOR FREE.

If you can't afford a car seat, contact your local children's hospital. Around the country several have started programs with manufacturers donating them. For a coupon that will give you a Century 1000 Convertible Carseat at wholesale ($42 vs. $80), contact your local Midas Muffler about its Project Safe Baby program. Midas will also give you a $42 voucher that can later be traded in for $42 off on brake work, making the car seat free.

You can also get a 42" shopping cart seat belt for $5 by contacting Safe-Strap, 180 Old Tappan Road, Old Tappan, N.J. 07675 or 201-767-7450.

Your local children's hospital is a good place to check for free classes on child safety issues like how to baby-proof your home and more. For-profit firms often charge $40 and up for such classes.

259 HELP AUDITING YOUR HOSPITAL BILLS.

More than 90% of all hospital bills have mistakes in them, yet they are so indecipherable that the average person has little chance of catching the mistakes—almost always in the hospital's favor. Get advice from the People's Medical Society ($20 annual fee; 462 Walnut St., Allentown, Pa. 18102; 610-770-

1670), a consumer advocacy group that puts out a bimonthly newsletter and will advise you on where to file complaints about overcharges.

260 FREE HEALTH ADVICE.

You can call Ask-a-Nurse at 800-535-1111 to be directed to a hospital in your area that will answer basic questions over the phone, free of charge. A handy booklet produced by the People's Medical Society lists hundreds of toll-free numbers. It is called Dial 800 for Health (800-624-8773; $5.95).

261 FREE HEALTH TESTS AND SEMINARS.

Hospitals and doctors, eager for business, are running dozens of free seminars on everything from breast cancer to allergies. You can also get free tests for blood pressure, cholesterol screening, mammograms and cancer screenings if you contact the local hospital's community education department. Free tests often coincide with months designated to call attention to a particular ailment. You usually only have to wait a few moments for testing, but call first: Some facilities take appointments.

If you donate blood to the Red Cross (800-450-4593), you will automatically be screened for AIDS and hepatitis, so don't waste money on those tests either. There is no income requirement for these freebies. The Centers for Disease Control (404-639-3311) sponsors these tests. For free information about AIDS, call the CDC at 800-342-2437.

262 MARRIAGE HELP.

Marriage counselors can be extremely expensive. So why not at least get a headstart on improving communication with some free help. For a free brochure called Marital Communications, send a SASE to Baylor College of Medicine, One Baylor Plaza, Room 176B, Houston, Texas 77030.

263 HELP TO QUIT SMOKING.

Plenty of entrepreneurs are hawking expensive treatments to rid you of an expensive habit. Get free advice from Out of the Ashes: Choosing a Method to Quit Smoking, a free booklet from the Centers for Disease Control and Prevention, Office on Smoking and Health, Mail Stop K-50, 4770 Buford Highway NE, Atlanta, Ga. 30341.

Chapter Five

HOME IMPROVEMENT

*From free jewelry appraisals to free information on
your nanny, here is your one stop-source for slashing
costs within your four walls.*

264 Free Appraisals or Estimates.

If you have a couple of prized heirlooms upon which you'd like a professional pronouncement, send a clear photo and a self-addressed envelope to one of the venerable auction houses: Christie's East, 219 E. 67th St., New York, N.Y. 10021, 212-606-0400 or 212-546-1000.
Sotheby's, 1334 York Ave., New York, N.Y. 10021, 212-606-7000. They will give you an estimate of what your treasure is worth (maximum of two requests).

Another good source is The Collector's Information Bureau (708-842-2200), which tracks market values of collectibles. It will provide you with handy books, The Collectibles Market Guide and Price Index ($26.70) and the Directory to Secondary Market Retailers ($14.70).

Oftentimes, dealers in particular periods will also give you a free quote in the hope that you will use their services.

265 Unbelievable Deals on Housing.

If you are good at fixing up properties, you can get incredible deals on houses through the U.S. Department of Housing and Urban Development. HUD homes are auctioned off at much lower than their value and may require as little as a $100 down payment. Call the HUD homeline 800-767-4483 and request A Home of Your Own, a free brochure that is a step-by-step buying guide for HUD homes.

266 Slash the Cost of Moving.

If you are moving yourself, rent your truck as far in advance as possible—especially if you are planning a move from May to September. Call around to compare prices, giving each company a chance to beat the other's price. Often, you can get the truck for 50% off the first price you were quoted. Also, ask about specials for moving during the week (weekends are more expensive) or a few days before or after the first of the month (peak time to move).

If you use Hertz, you may be able to use coupons from your frequent flyer memberships. Don't forget to check on insurance for your belongings while you're on the road. Ask your agent what your homeowner's policy will cover. You may need to get a rider to cover your belongings while they are in transit. The coverage offered by the moving companies traditionally pays out a mere pittance of what your items are actually valued at. Get a free guide on moving from the U.S. Postal Service or U-Haul. The post office guide includes several handy coupons with discounts on rental trucks and more.

267 FREE MOVING ADVICE.

Write Mayflower Transit, Inc., P.O. Box 107, Indianapolis, Ind. 46206 to get a free information kit on planning, scheduling and packing.

268 GET FREE GIFTS AND INFORMATION WHEN YOU MOVE.

Moving is one of the most stressful, costliest tasks we undertake. Yet most folks fail to reward themselves by letting a good, old-fashioned call from the Welcome Wagon International cheer them up. You have to let the Welcome Wagon know you're new in town. Local merchants supply Welcome Wagon, listed in the business white pages, with a plethora of gifts and coupons for newcomers. The one catch is that representatives insist on giving the goodies to you in person, but with all the coupons for free dry cleaning, meals, haircuts and more, the effort is probably worth it. In some larger metro areas, Welcome Wagon has competition, too, so you may get a double welcome.

269 FREE INFORMATION ON HAVING YOUR PROSPECTIVE HOME INSPECTED.

To make sure your home inspector is properly qualified, check with the American Society of Home Inspectors (85 W.

Algonquin Road, Arlington Heights, Ill. 60005 or 708-290-1919). The association can also give you good tips on what to expect. When you have the home inspected, go with the inspector and get one to two hours of expert advice on the most important things to fix in your home. Also, he or she can tell you additions you could make that would add the most value for your dollar. You can also get valuable information from the inspector on what other homes in the area are like.

At the end of the inspection, you'll be given a large book, filled with do-it-yourself tips on maintaining your home. Keep it and refer to it often. A comparable book would cost $25 or more from the bookstore.

270 FREE ADVICE ON HOME REMODELING.

Before you hire a contractor, you need to know what you're getting. Here are ways to check out a contractor:
National Association of the Remodeling Industry (4301 N. Fairfax Drive, Suite 310, Arlington, Va. 22203-1627 or 800-966-7601) has a brochure called How to Choose A Professional Remodeler as well as a list of NARI remodeling members in your area.

The Remodelers Council of the National Association of Home Builders, 1201 15th St. N.W., Washington, D.C. 20005-2800, 800-368-5242 ext. 212.

American Homeowner's Foundation, 6776 Little Falls Road, Arlington, Va. 22204 or 703-536-7776 ($7.95 for a six-page remodeling contract written from a consumer's perspective).

271 FREE HELP FOR HOUSEHUNTERS.

The Federal Trade Commission has produced several free publications on this topic, including: Mortgage Money Guide, Mortgage Servicing, Real Estate Brokers, Refinancing Your Home and Home Financing Primer. Write Public Reference, Room 130, Federal Trade Commission, Washington, D.C. 20580 or call 202-326-2222.

272 MAIL-ORDER DECORATING FOR DISCOUNTS UP TO 80%

Edgar B (800-255-6589) is the king of discounts on name brand furniture direct from manufacturers. The catalogs are filled with stylish choices. For more choices, write the Catawba County Chamber of Commerce (P.O. Box 1828, Hickory, N.C. 28603 or call 704-328-6111) for a free brochure listing more than 40 furniture outlets in North Carolina, which is the capital of furniture manufacturing in this country. Most offer mail-order service. Here is a sampling:

Mallory's, P.O. Box 1150, Jacksonville, N.C. 28541; 910-353-1828.

House Dressing Furniture, 2212 Battleground, Greensboro, N.C. 27408; 800-322-5850. Free brochure; more than 200 manufacturers.

Village Furniture House, 146 West Ave., Kannapolis, N.C. 28081; 704-938-9171.

For great buys on wallpaper and window treatments, try American Blind and Wallpaper Factory (800-735-5300), American Discount Wallcoverings (800-777-2737), Wells Interiors Inc. (800-547-8982), Windoware (800-426-7780) or Worldwide Wallcoverings & Blinds, Inc. (800-336-WALL).

To save on mattresses, call Dial-A-Mattress (800-MAT-TRES). For light fixtures, contact King's Chandelier Co. (910-623-6188); Golden Valley Lighting (800-735-3377 or 919-882-7330); Lamp Warehouse/New York Ceiling Fan Center (718-436-8500) or Luigi Crystal (215-338-2978).

For bed and bath linens, call Ezra Cohen Corp. (212-925-7800) or Harris Levy, Inc. (800-221-7750 or 212-226-3102). Best deals on carpets are found in Dalton, Ga. Contact Johnson's Carpets, Inc. (800-235-1079 or 404-277-2775) for 20-80% below retail.

To find out more about what's available, send $3 for the Great Catalog Guide to the Direct Marketing Association, 1111 19th St. N.W., Washington, D.C. 20036-3603.

273 FREE FIRE EXTINGUISHERS.

AmeriSpec (800-909-8090), a national home inspection chain, gives free first aid kits to customers during the summer months. During Fire Prevention Week in October, AmeriSpec hands out fire extinguishers.

274 STAINLESS PLACE SETTING FOR $1.

Watch for introductory offers from well-respected companies. Watchmakers, jewelry makers and others often run specials that allow you to sample their products for free or a tiny amount in the hope of making you a loyal customer. (The Wall Street Journal is a good place to look for such offers.) A recent offer from Oneida Stainless gave customers a choice of seven different styles of a 7-piece Oneida stainless place setting ($45 value) for $1. Contact Oneida Savings Plan, 125 Armstrong Road, Des Plaines, Ill. 60019; 708-298-3705.

275 FREE POSTERS FIT FOR FRAMING.

Each month the U.S. Postal Service sends all post offices a colorful poster featuring art from current stamps. These posters are free for the taking. Ask the manager of your local post office if you have your eye on a particular one. For your kids' room or playroom, ask your local athletic store to kick in a poster of Michael Jordan or other favorite athletic hero when you make a purchase.

276 FREE INFORMATION ON YOUR NANNY.

Nanny News is a bimonthly newsletter that gives solid advice on making the relationship with your childcare-giver work. You can get a free sample issue by calling 800-634-6266 (Hopewell, N.J.). You can also request a free copy of the In-Home Childcare Giver's Resource Guide. A year's subscription to the newsletter is $14.95.

277 PEACE OF MIND AT A BARGAIN RATE:

Check out your childcare worker's background. Any parent who has tried to hire someone to take care of a child knows how difficult checking references can be. Now you can easily and quickly have a detailed background (including the all-important criminal check) run on a potential caregiver for a reasonable price. The ChildCare Registry (Danville, Calif.; 800-227-0033 or 510-248-4100) delivers a national background check for a $140 fee + $8 handling.

278 GET A FREE ENERGY INSPECTION.

If your gas bill appears unusually high, contact your utility company. You may have a slow leak, and the utility company is one of the few companies left that makes free house calls. Most offer free energy savers, which include inspecting your home for energy-wasters and suggesting low-cost ways to reduce your heating and cooling costs and water usage.

While you're at it, check your phone bill for something called the wire maintenance charge. You're probably shelling out $2 or more for a service you're never going to need. Basically that's phone repair insurance that decrees that the phone company has to fix a problem with your line even if it's inside the house. Otherwise, you are responsible for fixing the phone if the problem occurs in the wiring inside. However, that's rare, and the phone company slips this charge past millions of consumers.

279 FREE CELLULAR PHONES.

Before you sign up for cellular service, check around and you'll likely at least get a free phone out of the deal. This business is ultra-competitive so it's easy to benefit. For example, just for signing up for monthly service, Peachtree Mobility in Atlanta was offering a choice of either an NEC transportable cellular phone or NEC handheld cellular phone.

280 FREE DECORATING ADVICE.

For a free decorating kit from La-Z Boy, call 800-MAKE-A-HOME. For a free consultation in your home or office with a decorator, call Decorating Den at 800-428-1366. The decorator will bring you a van full of samples for wallcoverings, draperies, carpeting, fabrics and furniture. Meanwhile, you have no obligation. Plus, the company often runs "buy one, get one free" specials. You'll also receive a free magazine with decorating advice just for calling.

281 FREE HELP IF YOUR CABLE COMPANY GIVES YOU STATIC.

If you don't believe you're being charged fairly for cable or have another dispute about the service, contact the Federal Communications Commission at 202-418-0200 to complain. The agency will send you a form to fill out detailing your beef. And it has been responsive to consumers' complaints about monopolistic cable companies.

282 FREE WATERMAN CENTURION PEN.

Before you toss an offer to test-drive a "pre-owned" Lexus, take a closer look. Just for giving the car a whirl, you get a free designer pen. Your junk mail probably contains some nifty treats like that. All you have to do to collect is steel yourself against high-pressure salespeople and enjoy the fruits of their come-ons. Some dealers are also offering $200-off coupons, so ask before you buy.

283 GET CAR CARE AT A DISCOUNT FROM TOP-NAME SERVICERS.

If you are on the road frequently, consider joining a club like AutoVantage (800-999-4CAR), which is similar to travel discount clubs. Membership ($49 a year) gets you 10-20% off auto repairs, maintenance and equipment at reputable dealers and servicers nationwide. It also gives you a nationwide towing service, emergency roadside assistance, trip routing and planning, key registration and a reporting service that helps you buy or lease a car. You also get discounts with every major car rental company.

284 KEEP AUTO MECHANICS HONEST.

Ask for the old part before paying for the repair. You might also consider using one of the new services called My Mechanic or Car Checkers of America that use diagnostic machines and provide you with a computer printout of problems the machine finds. Numerous investigations have found that consumers still suffer big ripoffs in this area, so be extremely cautious.

285 GET A BREAK FROM THE MANUFACTURER IF YOUR CAR IS A LEMON.

Automobile recalls are not always well publicized, especially if the defect is minor. If your car is continually breaking down, send a SASE with two stamps along with a letter with the make, model and year your car was manufactured, as well as the problem it's having. Contact: Center for Auto Safety, 2001 S St. N.W., Suite 410, Washington, D.C. 20009 or 202-328-7700. (If you have young children, ask for a free list of child safety seat recalls. They are one of the most commonly recalled items, yet only 10% of those recalled have been returned for repairs or replacement.) Another resource is the National

Highway Traffic Safety Administration Auto Safety Hotline at 800-424-9393.

One woman who bought a used Nissan van was dismayed when it continually broke down. The first dealer she complained to said she was stuck. However, after moving to a new state and complaining to another dealer she found out that the particular model she owned was known for having breakdowns and was on the verge of being recalled. Rather than making her wait for the official recall, the dealer wrote her a check for more than she had paid for the van in the first place.

Knowing if there is a documented problem can aid you in negotiating a better price, or you may even be offered a replacement vehicle. If you don't get satisfaction from the dealer, ask for customer service at the manufacturers. When the owner of a Ford Taurus that had a door that wasn't properly hinged, and thus destroyed the siding on his car, initially complained to a dealer, he was told he would have to pay the $300 to replace the side molding. After a call to the manufacturer, the dealer himself called to ask that the car be brought in and all the work was completed free of charge.

If you still aren't satisfied, you may consider arbitration with the car manufacturer:

Toyota or Lexus Vehicles, AutoSolve Manufacturers Arbitration Program, 1000 AAA Drive, Heathrow, Fla. 32746 or call the Council of Better Business Bureaus at 800-477-6583;

Ford Vehicles, Ford Consumer Appeals Board, 300 Renaissance Center, P.O. Box 43360, Detroit, Mich. 48243 or 800-392-3673;

General Motors, Saturn or Volkswagen Vehicles, Better Business Bureau Autoline; call your local BBB.

286 FREE BOOKS AND CDS.

If you live in a small to medium-sized town and consider yourself a good critic when it comes to the arts, check with your local newspapers—dailies and communities—and ask about doing a column. You would not believe the sheer volume of free books or CDs you will soon find yourself buried under if you can show publishers and record labels that you have any kind of audience at all.

287 HOME ELECTRONICS FOR 20-40% OFF.

You can get discounts on "factory serviced" electronics returned by customers. A great selection is found through the Damark catalog (800-729-9000).

288 FREE TICKETS TO EVENTS FOR KIDS.

If you work with underprivileged kids or someone you know does, contact Ticketmaster regarding its "Tickets for Kids" program. The nationwide company is giving away choice tickets to inner-city kids to everything from Disney on Ice to the Eagles.

289 FREE TOYS.

Parents magazine has a Child Development Toy Program that gives you a $9.95 toy for your baby for free. It also comes with a free guide on your child's development. Write: The Child Development Toy Program, P.O. Box 16722, Columbus, Ohio 43216-6722 to request an order card. There will also be a drawing for a $20,000 scholarship connected to this offer (ends 1/15/96).

290 FREE MAGAZINE FOR NEW PARENTS.

If you have a new baby, get American Baby magazine free for an entire year. It's a terrific magazine and often has good coupons. Write P.O. Box 53093, Boulder, Colo. 80322 or 303-604-1464.

291 FREE AMERICAN BABY BASKET.

Babies are expensive. So get a complimentary basket stuffed with samples and coupons from the best manufacturers by sending your name, address, baby's birthday and the hospital name, city and state to: American Baby Basket, Gift Headquarters, P.O. Box 734, New York, N.Y. 10113-0734.

292 FREE 35MM CAMERA WITH CARRYING CASE.

Just for trying a three-month membership for free with Buyers Advantage (through Signet Bank Card Center, P.O. Box 26030, Richmond, Va. 23276 or 800-553-4948), you get a free camera. These buying services can be a good deal if you are on the verge of purchasing small appliances, outfitting your home office or remodeling your home. Otherwise, you can still take advantage of the great freebies the credit card companies offer as a come-on, but you simply must remember to cancel the membership within the time limit specified. The companies count on your forgetting to dispute the $49 charge, which is refundable the first year.

293 OWNING A SPA.

If you've been thinking of buying a hot tub, but just aren't sure whether soaking at 104 degrees would agree with you, get a free guide called Owning a Spa. Call Lucite XL at 800-253-8881.

294 TAKING A BITE OUT OF CRIME.

The National Citizen's Crime Prevention Campaign (800-937-7383) is offering a free booklet called Stop the Violence, Start Something that gives advice on a wide range of crime prevention techniques. It also comes with an order form for more publications and products—some free.

295 SAVE 33% OFF A SEWING MACHINE.

Sewing is making a comeback. Send a SASE for a price quote on name brand machines to Singer Sewing Center of College Station, 1667 Texas Ave., College Station, Texas 77840 or call 800-338-5672.

296 ASK ABOUT DENT AND SCRATCH DISCOUNTS WHEN BUYING APPLIANCES.

Look at the display models and ask the salespeople about slightly damaged appliances. You can save 20-30% on perfectly good appliances. Indeed, a recent purchase of a "damaged" dryer saved $200 off the retail price. The scratch proved to be a smear of grease. Minor scratches can be covered quickly and easily by appliance paint. More major problems might require a visit from Surface Doctor (800-828-1227): a $30-40 repair vs. a $100-400 savings or more.

This strategy can work with other items as well—even in upscale stores. On a pair of children's cowboy boots at a ritzy store in Aspen, Colo., a customer asked for and got 20% off because of a slight imperfection in the boot.

297 GET FREE LIGHT BULBS AND MORE FROM YOUR POWER COMPANY.

Ask for an energy conservation check-up from your local utility. Most will come and do a free home inspection and give you a full report on what you can do to slash your utility bills. The inspector also often comes bearing gifts: a free insulating wrap for your water heater, free light bulbs and a free water-conserving shower head. Those items alone are worth close to $100, not to mention the energy savings they provide.

298 BOOK ON HOUSEHOLD INFORMATION.

Bristol-Myers Co. has compiled a 191-page book on household products, appliances, prescription drugs and more. For a free copy write Bristol-Myers Co. Consumer Information Dept., 345 Park Ave., New York, N.Y. 10022.

299 GREAT MOVIES FOR FREE.

Learning how to program your VCR doesn't have to be as painful as you think. Figure it out and then tape the terrific movies that are showing at inconvenient times for you and watch a free showing rather than spending your hard-earned bucks at the video store.

300 FREE RECIPES.

If you are always itching to whip up something new in the kitchen, there is no shortage of free sources. Many grocery stores now have an area in the front of the store with free recipe booklets and recipe cards. Companies often offer them, too. For instance, call Empire Chicken (800-367-4734) for a free 33-page chicken recipe book; Louis Kemp (800-522-1421) for seafood recipes.

301 GET A WEEK'S WORTH OF FREE CHILDCARE.

If you have your child in a formal program, you may be surprised to learn that most preschools will give you a free week's worth of care once your child has been enrolled a year. You have to ask. Schools don't go out of their way to let you know about this benefit.

302 USE A HOME DELIVERY SERVICE TO SAVE 10-30% OFF YOUR GROCERY BILL.

Larger families who have members who are meat lovers should check into services that deliver your grocery order to your home. They specialize in selling frozen meats and seafood in bulk and therefore cut prices by cutting out the middleperson (the grocer). A representative will come to your home and spend about 45 minutes with you finding out your likes and dislikes. For signing up you'll be awarded a welcome like 10 prime beef fillets. If you don't like the service, you still get to keep the welcoming gift. Although the service will also offer to bring you staples like toilet paper, some complain that prices are not as good on such items and suggest sticking with the meats only. Look in your phone book. One is Colorado Prime (800-365-2404), based in Great Neck, N.Y. If you sign up with a five-month food order, you can pay by the month with no finance charges. The rub is that these companies may try to sell you a small freezer—at a much higher price than you could get on your own.

303 GET A BREAK ON BABY NECESSITIES.

New parents are often shocked at the prices on baby food, diapers and formula. If you are loyal to a certain brand, call the toll-free number once a month to make a comment on the product, and you'll be rewarded with a fistful of coupons. Also, be wary of convenience. For example, the small cans and jars of apple juice packaged and sold next to the baby food are an outrageous ripoff. Steer clear and instead buy apple juice in a gallon container. It's the same product at one-fourth the price.

304 FREE PETS.

Avoid pet stores—especially those at the mall—like the plague. You'll likely get a healthier animal for free from the shelter. (You may be asked for a small donation to cover vaccinations.) Pets sold commercially are often not the pick of the litter and have been subjected to poor health conditions, which can mean big vet bills for you later on.

305 FREE MUNCHIES FOR FIDO.

The following pet food manufacturers will send you free samples or coupons for dog and cat food.
Hills Science Diet 800-445-5777

Iams & Eukanuba 800-525-4267 or 800-255-4738
Nature's Recipe 800-843-4008
Natural Life Pet Products 800-367-2391
Purina 800-PRO-PLAN or 800-323-4ONE
For example, Purina will send you a 10 oz. free sample Fit & Trim adult dog food. Call or write to: Purina, P.O. Box 15344, Mascoutah, Ill. 62224.
NutroMax 800-833-5330. Pet stores, veterinarian clinics and pet shows are all also good sources of free samples. Just ask.

306 GET WOOD FOR FREE AND MORE CLASSIFIED SURPRISES.

In your local community newspaper, you may find free classi-fieds advertising items and services for barter. You'll find things like lumber, appliances and firewood that companies would rather give away than pay to have carted. According to Amy Dacyczyn, author of Tightwad Gazette (Leeds, Maine 04263 or 207-524-7962 for a free sample; $12 for a year's subscription), a monthly newsletter on great deals, one woman who respond-ed to a national chain's ad got a brand new $600 range that ended up needing only a $15 repair.

307 REPLACEMENT PARTS FOR KIDS' TOYS FOR FREE.

Before you junk your child's beloved toy because of a lost piece, try writing the manufacturer. They will typically send customers the lost item. Some like Fisher Price even put out catalogs for replacement parts: Write Fisher Price Toys, Consumer Affairs, 636 Girard Ave., E. Aurora, N.Y. 14052-1880 or call 800-432-5437.

308 MAKE YOUR DRY CLEANER PAY IF THERE'S A PROBLEM.

Before you entrust your designer wardrobe to a cleaner, ask the owner or manager what the policy is if a problem arises. Look for a dry cleaner that stands by its work. Keep all tickets and carefully check your order when it is returned. If an item is missing, ask to be fully compensated for the item. One New York City dry cleaner wrote out a $650 check for a new designer suit that turned up missing after being put in for alterations. The customer had the receipt and the dry cleaning ticket.

If you aren't happy with the job, request a report from the International Fabricare Institute, 12251 Tech Road, Silver Spring, Md. 20904, 800-638-2627. If the manufacturer is at fault, most cleaners will advise you on how to get in touch with the proper company to get a refund. Other options: small claims court or your Better Business Bureau's Dry Cleaning Arbitration Program.

Women are often charged more for cleaning. If you find that at your cleaner, register your complaint and look for a cleaner who does not discriminate or who can clearly explain reasons for higher charges.

309 GET CHINA AND CRYSTAL FOR 65% OFF.

You can get discounts on name brands like Lenox, Mikasa, Gorham, Christian Dior, Royal Doulton and Waterford through several discounters who specialize in mail-order. Call:

Barrons 800-538-6340

The China Warehouse 800-321-3212

Midas 800-368-3153

Ross-Simons Jewelers 800-556-7376

Or you can get Tyrone crystal (similar to Waterford for much less) by calling the Irish Crystal Company & Classic Linens, Inc. (800-947-2863; 3168 Peachtree Road, N.E., Atlanta, Ga. 30305). The company will send you a free catalog featuring its Irish linens and imported crystal.

310 HOUSEPLANTS FOR NEXT TO NOTHING.

Call companies that rent plants to corporations. They often sell 'used' plants for a song. Look in the Yellow Pages under plants.

311 CHEAP SECURITY.

More and more people are spending hundreds and even thousands of dollars on home security systems. Surveys have shown that even stickers warning of such a system can be a deterrent to opportunistic burglars. Spend a few dollars for the stickers and skip the $1,000 and up you'd shell out for a security system.

312 UNUSUAL WAYS TO GET FURNITURE FOR MUCH LESS.

You can contact builders and ask where they sell the contents of their model homes. Check in the Yellow Pages for model home clearance centers. You can get terrific buys that have been professionally selected by some of your town's top designers who are hip to what's selling houses these days. Another source for great furniture buys is furniture rental places like Aaron Rents. Call and ask when the store's clearance sales are held. You can have barely used furniture at less than half what it would have cost you new.

313 GET FREE APPRAISALS.

When remodeling or fixing up your house, let companies come to you and save the wear and tear on your car. For instance, companies that organize your closets, like the Closet Factory and California Closet, send a consultant who will spend an hour or so giving you a free consultation—even offering a free rough sketch outlining their suggestions for your overstuffed spaces. Consider their professional suggestions and then you may want to adapt them yourself, buying the necessary items at a discounter. Carpet cleaning, furniture repair, resurfacing, decorating companies all routinely give free estimates. Compare prices and quality of work and don't feel pressured to sign on because the salesperson came to you.

New technologies have made these services even more convenient. For example, Floor Coverings International

(800-877-9933) has a computer that shows prospective clients what a room would look like with the flooring of their choice. Using a patented process, Furniture Medic (800-877-9933) can repair a whole roomful of furniture in your home or at your business within a few hours with no messy drips or smells.

314 FREE LAND FOR ADVENTUROUS SOULS.

More than 30 states have land available for free to people who agree to certain terms. For instance, one family scored 20 acres in Alaska on which they built a home out of logs cut from the land they had been given. Total out-of-pocket costs: $30,000. Value of the land and house: $80,000. Contact the local office of the Bureau of Land Development.

You can also get free room and board in some of the nation's most pristine surroundings by working as a volunteer for the National Park Service.

315 FREE DESIGN OF AN ENERGY CONSERVATION SYSTEM.

The Department of Energy provides the Energy Efficiency and Renewable Energy Clearinghouse (800-428-2525), which gives you free information on conservation and answers your queries. The division will design an energy conservation system for your heating and cooling system at no cost to you.

316 SLASH ELECTRIC BILLS BY USING FLUORESCENT RATHER THAN INCANDESCENT BULBS.

Fluorescent bulbs use 75% less electricity, and last 10-14 times longer. You can also save by buying long-lasting bulbs directly from your local utility.

317 GET FREE ENVELOPES.

Save on envelopes by using FedEx or Express Mail envelopes for mailings rather than buying your own. The hard cardboard serves as good protection as long as you don't overstuff them.

If you write overseas, buy airmail stationery with postage and get the envelopes for free. However, do not use company's pre-paid envelopes to try to send them somewhere else. They have a bar-code on them that makes the post office automatically send them to the addresss the company originally intended.

318 GET FREE SHOES FOR THE FAMILY.

A real find by Jackie Iglehart, author of The Penny Pincher newsletter (call 800-41PENNY or 516-724-1872 or send $1 and a SASE for a sample to P.O. Box 809-E, Kings Park, N.Y. 11754), is the Shoe Testers Association (STA). After paying a $25 membership fee, you can get name brand athletic shoes for adults and children for about $10 a pair. Fill out a survey about how you like them, and in return you get a coupon for $10 off your next order, meaning free shoes. You can also buy seconds of popular manufacturers through the STA. Contact the STA at: 2155 Chesnee Highway, Spartanburg, S.C. 29303 or 803-583-1002/fax 803-583-0086.

319 FREE SEED CATALOGS.

Get free mail-order catalogs from top seed companies. For excellent vegetables, contact

Burpee Seed Co. (800-888-1447).

Park Seed Co. (800-845-3369).

Wayside Gardens (800-845-1124) specializes in trees and shrubs.

White Flower Farm (203-496-9600) is great for full-grown flowering plants. Each company offers a one-year replacement plan if you aren't satisfied with the results.

320 FREE CHRISTMAS TREES.

Through a non-profit organization, you can get a free permit to cut a Christmas tree for your own use through the Bureau of Land Management. Or individuals can cut a tree with a $10 permit from the bureau, which also gives permission to collect seedlings and cactuses if they are in abundance. Contact your local office (permits come from the field offices) or the U.S. Department of the Interior, Bureau of Land Management, Division of Forestry, 1849 C St. N.W., Washington, D.C. 20240 or 202-452-7755.

321 FREE MULCH FOR YOUR GARDEN AND FLOWER BEDS.

Check with the places that chip Christmas trees each year. For example, Home Depot sets up piles where consumers can come and help themselves. You'll also find such giveways at designated areas in city parks.

322 SAVE A TREE.

Woodworking shops and cabinet shops will often save their hardwood waste for you. Saves them carting charges and gives you free firewood.

323 FREE FIREWOOD.

If you need wood to keep your home fires burning, for a $35 fee you can get a license from the National Park Service that allows you to take unlimited wood from naturally fallen trees in state and national parks. With a cord of wood running at $100 or more, the savings quickly add up.

324 FREE LAWN CARE ANALYSIS.

Another business that's extremely competitive is caring for your lawn. By calling a few companies, you can get plenty of expert advice on problems you're having, and you'll wind up with a good price by shopping around. Ask for a free analysis of what you should be doing to get your lawn in tip-top shape.

325 GO TO BIG EXHIBITION SHOWS.

Attending supershows geared to parents, gardeners, home-owners, boat aficionados, car enthusiasts and the like can net you great free gifts and invaluable information. At shows like the Philadelphia Flower Show (215-625-8253), look for seed giveaways and free lectures by the nation's top landscapers. At home shows, you can get free demonstrations of all kinds of products and valuable coupons. For example, you might find one that will give you $200 off your home appraisal. It's a great way to get on mailing lists to put yourself in the loop for more freebies.

326 FREE REPLACEMENTS FOR DAMAGED LANDSCAPING.

If your landscaping is a masterpiece, you can get compensated for damages on your homeowner's insurance if disaster strikes, according to the International Society of Arboriculture (217-355-9411, Savoy, Ill.). You might also be able to claim compensation through the Internal Revenue Service, since landscaping adds to the value of your home. To be eligible, though, you must regularly photograph your property, keep receipts for plant purchases and maintenance and have it appraised by a professional landscaper. That documentation can take the sting out of a natural disaster like wind damage.

327 LANDSCAPE FOR LESS.

One of the most expensive housing upgrades you can make is landscaping. But landscape designers often offer free consultations. Ask for it. Let the person know your budget and what you'd like incorporated in the design. Make notes and sketches yourself, tape record the conversation as you walk the property, or pay a small fee (roughly $100-200) for a rough sketch done by the landscape designer. For a free referral to a landscape architect, call the American Society of Landscape Architects (202-686-2752).

328 SEEDS FOR FREE.

Pay attention to the gardening section of your newspaper. You'll often see ads for free seeds or plant and seed exchanges (you swap your oversupply for what you want). Seed Exchangers ($1.50 for a sample issue), P.O. Box 10, Burnips, Mich. 49314-0010, includes a seed swap listing in each month's issue.

Thompson & Morgan (Horticulture Dept., P.O. Box 1308, Jackson, N.J. 08527-0308; 800-274-7333 or 908-363-2225) annually seeks testers for trials of its flowers and vegetables ($20 application fee for both programs). If your application cuts the mustard, you'll be shipped about $40 worth of seeds. Your end of the bargain is documenting growth from germination to maturity. Send in your application by May to meet the cutoff date for the growing season during which you'd like to plant.

Seeds Blum, which specializes in hard-to-find seeds, has a smaller-scale testing program. The company asks $3 for a catalog for a new customer. The catalog lists 700 vegetables, 300 flowers and 100 herbs varieties and provides a tremendous amount of information (Seeds Blum, HC 33, Box 2057, Boise, Idaho 83706, 208-342-0858 or fax 208-338-5658).

Shepherd's Garden Seeds (30 Irene St., Torrington, Conn. 06790, 203-482-3638 or fax 203-482-0532) has a trial gardener offer in the catalog. At the end of the year, you send in information sheets for each packet and report on anything you like. In return, you'll get one free packet for each five you reported on for the next year. When someone gives especially good information, you may be contacted to test seeds that aren't even available to the public yet.

Another offer from Le Jardin du Gourmet, P.O. Box 75-GD, St. Johnsbury Ctr., Vt. 05863 (send $1 for postage and handling) sends a five-packet herb sampler. It comes with a catalog with recipes and instructions on herb growing.

329 PRICE BREAKS ON BULBS AND ROSES.

Breck's (U.S. Reservation Center, 6523 North Galena Road, Peoria, Ill. 61632; 800-722-9069) offers bulbs shipped directly from Holland for 55% off retail if you order early for fall planting. The company also ships a dozen or more crocus bulbs for free when you order $30 or more. Every order nets a free book on bulbs. Bulbs for at least 20% off retail can be had from Dutch Gardens (P.O. Box 200, Adelphia, N.J. 07710 or call 800-818-3861 or 908-780-2713 for a free catalog).

Get antique roses (more pest resistant than most hybrids) from The Antique Rose Emporium (Rt. 5 Box 143, Brenham, Texas 77833; 409-836-9051 or 409-836-0928). You'll wind up spending a lot less to care for antique or "old" roses, as they are sometimes called. The mail-order company produces a breathtaking, full-color catalog. Or if you are in the neighborhood (between Austin and Houston) in late fall, attend its free, three-day symposium on roses during which speakers from all over the world expound on roses and their care.

330 FREE TREE REMOVAL.

If you have a tree that needs to be removed, some outfits will pay you for the privilege rather than the other way around. Call woodworking shops and sawmills listed in the Yellow Pages. A few phone calls can save you the $500 and up that an arborist would charge to remove the tree.

331 THINK TWICE BEFORE YOU DIAL FOR THE REPAIRMAN.

Major appliance repairs are one of the biggest ripoffs out there. First, use the free home repair book typically provided by your home inspector when you purchased your house. If at all possible, see if you can take the leaky pipe or defective part into your hardware store or do-it-yourself clinic before you shell out big bucks for a repairman. You may find a $3 hose solves the problem that you were about to pay a $60 service call to fix.

These days retailers are scrambling for ways to please you and will often try to solve problems on the spot. Or ask friends for references and cultivate a relationship with an all-around handyman. Rates will often be about $15 an hour—far below what you'd pay a repairman from a retail store. Worse, several exposés have recently shown that, like auto mechanics, appliance repairman often inflate charges and fail to make the proper repairs.

332 FREE ENERGY SAVERS.

Clean your air-conditioner filters or vents once a month. If they get dirty, your heating and cooling system has to work much harder, using more electricity. Bonus: Less dust and fewer respiratory problems requiring expensive antihistamines.

Pack your freezer. The more frozen goods are in there, the colder the food stays and less energy is required.

Do all of your laundry in one day. Once a dryer heats up, it takes less electricity or gas to keep it toasty.

333 SLASH ENERGY COSTS 20% OR MORE.

Buy and install a programmable water heater control and thermostat computer. Total cost for both: about $100. But your bills will dwindle significantly. One family saw their power bill go to one-third what their neighbors' bills were after installing a computer on thermostats in both the upstairs and downstairs of their home. More tips:

Keep your water heater snug with an insulating blanket. Otherwise, about 10% of your energy bill is radiating into the surrounding air. Fix faucet drips immediately. Wrap pipes with insulation. Builders often cut corners by skipping the insulation on unheated spaces like garages and crawl spaces. Do it yourself and you'll likely be shocked at how much you'll save on the power bill. Call Owens-Corning Fiberglass at

800-438-7465 and ask for its free Homeowner's Guide to Insulation and Energy Savings.

Get 20% off heating oil by having your tank filled in the summer rather than during the fall rush.

Find out if your area offers off-peak usage discounts. You can save $200 or so off your bill annually by simply running your dishwasher, washer and dryer at the times requested by the power company.

Buy ceiling fans with reversible motors and use them all year long to cool in the summer and help push heat back down in a room. They don't use much electricity, yet fans enable you to put thermostats at a energy-conserving level.

Call the Department of Energy's Efficiency and Renewable Energy Clearinghouse at 800-523-2929 with questions about energy conservation and for free information and resources.

334 THE AVERAGE U.S. WEDDING COSTS $18,000.

Here are ways to slash costs. Consider a weeknight wedding to get a lower rate on the space. Call your local chamber of commerce or one in a nearby rural town to get a list of parks, country inns, historic mansions and other possibilities that often beat the prices of traditional churches and synagogues by a country mile. Another option is to rent an elegant hall, library or chapel on a college campus.

Garden club members may agree to design flower arrangements for you free of charge in return for a small donation. Local nurseries sometimes will lend plants, shrubs and trees for decorations. If you plan a holiday wedding, the church or synagogue will likely already be decorated. Or you may want to substitute silk flowers that you can use later on.

Order your cake from a local vocational school that teaches culinary arts. The Discount Bridal Service (800-874-8794), a personal buying service for brides, gives you discounts on invitations (use thermograph rather than engraved) and nationally advertised bridal gowns (20-40% off). For mail-order shopping, call JC Penney Bridal Catalogue (800-527-8345).

For the honeymoon, all-inclusive packages typically save you 20-30%—although on the surface they may appear more expensive—plus you don't have the hassle of pulling out cash or credit cards at every turn. Always mention that you'll be on your honeymoon. You'll usually be feted with an extra bottle of champagne, a special breakfast for two, T-shirts and other goodies. If you are a member of an alumni club or other organization, find out if travel discounts apply.

The Bridal Registry Book by Leah Ingram ($12.95; Contemporary Books, 800-621-1918) lists the names and, in most cases, toll-free phone numbers of 116 stores all over the country where you can register for gifts and make it easy on your family and your friends.

335 GET ORGANIZED.

Since everybody knows time is money, you owe it to yoursef to get organized. For free help locating an organizational whiz, contact the National Association of Professional Organizers (1033 La Posada Drive, Suite 220, Austin, Texas 78752-3880; 512-206-0151.)

336 CUT COSTS BY CUTTING THE CLUTTER OUT OF YOUR LIFE.

Paying bills late because they've gotten buried in a stack of junk mail can cost you $15-20 per bill in penalties. If you divide your mortgage payment by the number of square feet in your house, you can figure out how much it costs you to store junk. And if you've moved unusable items even once, you've wasted a lot of money. With lives that seem to get busier and busier, papers and junk can quickly pile up. Pick up a copy of

Clutter Control (Good Advice Press, 800-255-0899; $6.99) for inspiration. Then call the Salvation Army or some other charity and donate as much as possible to get a tax break. (Actually, the Salvation Army now lists typical values of items commonly donated on the back of the receipt it gives you.) If President Clinton's used underwear rates $11 a pair, think what you could get. Terrific tip: After you've raked in the dough from a yard sale to ditch your clutter, take the remainder directly to a local charity and get a receipt for your donation. Otherwise, you might be tempted to bring your trash back into your house.

337 SAVE YOUR TIES WITH TIE PROTECTOR SPRAY.

You'll nix exorbitant dry-cleaning bills and save expensive ties by springing for a $2 can of protective spray.

338 FREE(DOM) FROM JUNK MAIL.

If you're tired of opening the stuff, you don't have to contact senders individually. Just one letter to the Direct Marketing Association Mail Preference Service, P.O. Box 9008, Farmingdale, N.Y. 11735-9008, will make that extra bulk disappear from your mailbox in about 90 days. If you need further help, call 212-768-7277.

339 RECYCLE FOR FREE.

Although in some communities, recycling spots have begun charging for the privilege, you can still find many businesses eager to help you in your quest for friendship with the earth. PostNet International offers free recycling of the plastic peanuts that come with packages. Many gas stations and tune-up shops accept used oil from do-it-yourselfers. Just one gallon of used oil can contaminate up to 1 million gallons of water. If you can't locate a taker, call the Environmental Protection

Agency (EPA) at 800-424-9346 and request a free pamphlet, How to Set Up a Local Program to Recycle Used Oil. While you're at it, you can also request the EPA's free newsletter on environmental waste. Many grocery stores accept plastic and paper bags for recycling.

340 Guide on Keeping Tires Longer Safely.

Request the Consumer Tire Guide from the Consumer Information Center, Pueblo, Colo. 81009. Send a SASE and 50 cents. Take the time to have your tires rotated. Better brands will last 20,000 miles longer if you rotate them. However, many consumers do not remember to do this task.

341 How Not to Get Taken on a Magic Carpet Ride.

Buying a high-quality oriental rug can be tricky business for a novice. The business is rife with people peddling less than desirable imitations that will quickly lose their looks. Get the scoop on the real deal with a free brochure called The Mystique of Oriental Rugs, from the Oriental Rug Retailers of America, 1600 Wilson Blvd., Suite 905, Arlington, Va. 22209.

342 Pocket Mechanic.

To get an easy-to-read chart that helps you determine the cause of your car's trouble, send a SASE, business-sized envelope to Bottom Line/Personal, "When Your Car Won't Start," P.O. Box 736, Springfield, N.J. 07081. Keep it in your glove compartment.

343 Flower Arrangements for Free.

Okay. Another tip from The Penny Pincher. This one isn't for the squeamish, but on an almost daily basis, funeral homes and hospitals ditch hundreds of dollars worth of flowers. Often families can't possibly deal with all the bouquets. Call the funeral home (or hospital) and ask if they have flowers they would like to be rid of. You can use the bouquets in your own home, donate them to your church or give them away to friends. Just make sure condolences are removed.

344 FREE GOURMET COFFEE.

Join the Brothers Club Gourmet for free and get free coffee samples, a newsletter, coupon and a coffee accessories catalog. Call 800-284-5776 or write P.O. Box 812124, Boca Raton, Fla. 33841-2124 for a membership form.

345 CHECK THE COMPETITION WHEN YOU MOVE TO A NEW PLACE.

Trumpet your arrival to anyone who might have a great handout to welcome you. Although most folks have heard of Welcome Wagon, you may not know that the venerable oldster has competition in many metropolitan areas. If you don't get called upon, check with the local chamber and see if there are any other welcoming committees. Metro Newcomer Service is a popular one, for example. Your packet will likely have offers of free haircuts, dry cleaning, pizza, grooming for your pet and more.

Chapter Six

ALL BUSINESS

Here's the scoop on "brand used" computers,
tinier telephone bills, business advice and even financing.

346 FREE GUIDE TO BUYING A BUSINESS.

If you are buying or selling your business, you can get a free consultation from VR Business Brokers. If you are a potential buyer, call 800-377-8722 for a free booklet. (VR Business Brokers, Inc. 1151 Dove, Suite 100, Newport Beach, Calif. 92660-2805, 714-975-1100 or fax 714-975-1940).

347 FREE ADVICE ON SETTING UP A SELF-INSURANCE PLAN.

For a free membership package that advises you on whether self-insuring would work for your company, contact the Self-Insurance Institute of America, Inc., 17300 Red Hill Ave., Suite 100, Irvine, Calif. 92714; 800-851-7789.

348 ONE-FIFTH OFF LEASE PRICE OF A GM CAR.

Small business owners who lease even one car are eligible for a special program called FleetPlan, if they have the American Express Corporate Card. FleetPlan gives small business owners a big players' break, slashing 20% off the lease price for the car. Call 800-451-3796. To get free advice on whether leasing makes sense for you in the first place, write for A Consumer Guide to Vehicle Leasing, the Federal Trade Commission, Public Reference Branch, 6th St. and Pennsylvania Ave. N.W., Room 130, Washington, D.C. 20580 or call 202-326-2222. Another source: Ryder Systems (800-RYDER-OK) produces free booklets on full-service leasing and commercial rentals.

You can also get Expert Lease ($49.95), a computer program that compares the costs of leasing and buying. Contact Chart Software, 2700 E. Bay Drive, Suite 201, Largo, Fla. 34641.

For a free copy of Leasing Made Easy, call 800-LEASE-11.

349 FREE INFORMATION ON WORKPLACE HAZARDS.

More and more folks are suffering from carpal tunnel syndrome, poor indoor air quality and back problems from sitting all day. For free booklets or a recorded message on these topics, contact the National Institute for Occupational Safety and Health (4676 Columbia Parkway, Cincinnati, Ohio 45226; 800-356-4674).

350 FREE TECHNICAL EXPERTISE.

Are you a technophobe often in need of a technohero? Request a free copy of the Technical Assistance Directory, Center for Environmental Research Information, U.S. Environmental Protection Agency, 26 West Martin Luther King Drive, Cincinnati, Ohio 45268; 513-569-7562.

351 FREE ADVICE ON GOING PUBLIC AND INVESTING.

Company going gangbusters? Start by contacting the Securities and Exchange Commission for free information on what it takes to go public. One helpful booklet is Q&A: Small Business and the SEC. Other frequently requested publications are What Every Investor Should Know and Invest Wisely. Write the Securities and Exchange Commission Publications Section, 450 5th St. N.W., Washington, D.C. 20549. Call 202-942-8088 for recorded information.

352 LOW-COST LANGUAGE SERVICES.

Hiring interpreters can be extremely pricey. If you are in business and need to talk to a client, there is low-cost help easily accessible that few people know about: AT&T Language Line Services. (Call 800-752-6096 for more information.) An operator will connect you within seconds to someone who can translate in more than 140 languages. Then you pay a per minute rate ($4.15-7.25). If you frequently call overseas and have a need for translation services, consider being a sub-scriber, which will make your rates $2.20-2.60 a minute. Call the sales office at 800-752-0093. Ask about a special promotion that waives the $200 sign-up fee and gives you your first month of service free (up to a $150 value).

353 FREE INSURANCE COMPARISONS FOR CONSUMERS AND BUSINESS OWNERS.

Quotesmith Corporation (800-556-9393) offers a free insurance price comparison service. With this handy service you call and give your parameters. Within 24 hours, the company faxes or mails you a comprehensive report showing the names of every qualifying policy, the latest A.M. Best rating of each company, the initial rate guarantees of every policy and the premiums sorted by price. The service is available for individual term life, medical insurance for individuals and families, group medical for businesses with up to 100 employees, single premium tax-deferred annuities, long-term care and Medicare supplement.

Another good source is INSurance INFOrmation, Inc. (23 Route 134, South Dennis, Mass. 02660; 800-472-5800). You pay a $50 fee and get guaranteed quotes on five of the lowest price term life insurance policies suited to your needs. Or the company will examine your existing policy and come up with a better price, or it will refund your money. Term insurance prices may vary by as much as 300%, so a service like this one can easily save you a great deal of money.

The following companies also give you free information with no obligation on solid life insurance companies:
Direct Insurance Services (9191 Town Centre Drive, Suite 280, San Diego, Calif. 92122; 800-622-3699) looks over 160 term life companies and gives you the three best quotes.
InsuranceQuote Services, Inc. (3200 North Dobson Road, Building C, Chandler, Ariz. 85224; 800-972-1104 or fax 602-

831-8139) gives quotes of the five lowest cost but high quality (meaning an A or better rating from A.M. Best) companies that sell term life insurance. It deals with 50 companies.

SelectQuote (800-343-1985 or fax 800-436-7000) gives quotes on five low-cost, term life insurance policies when you give your specific information. It deals with 16 different companies.

TermQuote (send your name, date of birth, amount of coverage desired and whether you smoke to: 3445 South Dixie Drive, Dayton, Ohio 45439 or call 800-444-TERM) delivers three to five quotes on term or life insurance. It monitors 75 companies.

354 SLASH HEALTH INSURANCE COSTS.

If you are self-employed, see if your local chamber of commerce has started health insurance for a group of small business people. You can often save more than half the premiums by joining with others. If you are turned down for coverage, you have 30 days to dispute it and can question the reasons. If you disagree with the logic and show improved health, you may qualify after all. Another option: the National Association for the Self-Employed, 2121 Precinct Line Road, Hurst, Texas 76054 or 800-827-9990.

Make sure you aren't doubly insured through both your work and your spouse. Figure out who has the best policy and stick with that one. The one exception: Don't drop either insurance policy right before a child is born even if you discover you are doubly covered. If your child is born with medical problems, you may need the additional coverage.

355 PUT TOGETHER GROUPS TO GET A BIG DISCOUNT.

Large companies learned a long time ago that they can throw their weight around. But small business owners have clout, too. If you have employees, consider starting a wellness program and cut a deal with a local health club to get membership at a reduced rate for yourself and your staff. The same strategy works if you are a member of a special interest group. Figure out what you'd like to have and convince the gang of the benefits. You can even get the same results by putting together a neighborhood buying group or other group that wields dollar clout.

356 Cut Your Phone Bill 20-40% by Shopping for Six-Second Billing.

Most companies bill you in one-minute increments. But if you work from home or run a small, growing company, shop around for a service that will bill you in six-second increments. Over the course of the year, you'll save hundreds of dollars.

Allnet 800-783-2020. Allnet Clear Value; flat rate of 17 cents a minute domestically. It bills in six-second increments after a minimum of 18 seconds. Allnet also offers validating codes to allow small business people to easily identify billable calls.

AT&T 800-222-0400. Ask about special deals on toll-free numbers; you can get one for as little as $5 a month plus usage. If you work from home, sign on with AT&T's True Rewards as a residence. Business rates are significantly higher.

MCI 800-444-2222. After the first month with MCI, your statement will give a detailed cost comparison between billing under your old long distance company and MCI. Friends and Family gives 30% off all calls for residential customers and anyone called who also uses MCI qualifies for 50% off.

LDDS Worldcom 800-275-0200. The fourth largest long distance company doesn't advertise, but it has fiber optics, calling cards and the other features of the behemoths. For small and mid-size businesses, Easy Answer gives a flat rate of 15.5 cents per minute during the day nationwide; after 5 p.m. it falls to 12.4 cents. Ask about long-term contracts and the rates go even lower. Residential customers are 10 cents from 8 a.m. to 5 p.m.

Frontier Long Distance 800-836-8080. Has a sliding scale of discounts for residents with discounts up to 30%; Common Sense is geared to small business owners; or with Simplicity, you get the six-second increment billing.

Sprint 800-877-4646. Ask about Business Sense.

357 CONTACT YOUR LOCAL POST OFFICE TO GET THE INSIDER'S SCOOP ON SLASHING MAIL COSTS.

No matter what size business you have, you can probably save on mailings. But you need a guide through the maze of regulations. The U.S. Postal Service has now set up Business Centers in most metropolitan areas across the nation to advise folks on saving money. The Mail Flow Planning System (a free IBM disk) shows you how to calculate discounts on any class of mail. Call 800-238-3150 to get the instructions. You can also get free copies of Designing Business Letter Mail and Addressing for Success at the Business Center.

358 CUT YOUR COMMUTING COSTS BY 20% A WEEK.

If you haven't already, check into telecommuting to work one or two days a week. If you are the boss, you'll probably find you can get a surprising amount of work done. Employers likewise are finding telecommuting workers' output often exceeds that of workers in the office by 20%, according to LINK Resources (800-722-5335), a New York-based research firm specializing in the economic impact of emerging technologies. Employers save on office overhead and less absenteeism. Technology makes staying in constant touch with the office possible.

359 BEFORE YOU MAKE A MOVE, FIND OUT WHAT FREEBIES AWAIT.

If you own your own business, consider moving to a new state or city. Call the economic or business development office and give them your wish list. Many states now—like Mississippi, Wyoming and South Carolina to name a few—are bending over backwards to attract businesses. You'll get a free cost analysis of what the move would mean for your company. You may also get waivers on sewer and water permits; huge tax breaks; breaks on utilities and savings on workers' compensation, health insurance and more. And when the local government of your current locale finds out that you are considering moving, it will sometimes ante up great deals that you would never have known about otherwise. The Right Choice Inc., Salem, Mass. (800-872-2294) compares cost-of-living and cost-of-doing-business for individuals and businesses.

360 SLASH THE COSTS OF BUSINESS MEETINGS—AND IMPRESS.

Want to impress clients? Buy a membership for the airline club that has the fanciest layout at your local airport. Conduct meetings in the plush surroundings with free drinks at your beck and call. Entrepreneur Michael Katz, founder of New Jersey-based Cenogenics, a medical testing kit firm that does more than half its business overseas, does exactly that. He has saved thousands of travel dollars and time by offering to meet busy clients at the Newark International Airport and then graciously whisking them to a club.

361 BUY USED COMPUTERS.

With technology changing so quickly and computer prices dropping like rocks, "used" may make more sense. Some of the largest national firms that specialize in used computer sales are Boston Computer Exchange (617-542-4414), American Computer Exchange (404-250-0050) and United Computer Exchange (404-612-1205).

If you don't know what to do with your own outdated computer, consider donating it for a big tax break rather than selling it for a song. The National Cristina Foundation (800-274-7846) will match your computer equipment with a needy disabled person or disadvantaged student. Once you ship it, the foundation will then send you a sheet stating the value of your gift.

362 FREE ADVICE FOR ENTREPRENEURS.

You may be a maverick in your business, but getting input never hurts. The Center for Entrepreneurial Management (212-633-0060) produces plenty of valuable information for cash-crunched business starters. Of course, the Small Business Administration's Answer Desk (800-8ASK-SBA) yields valuable free information. (Be prepared, however, to wade through lengthy electronic menus to get what you want.) Women's Business Development Center (312-853-3477) provides entrepreneurial training, resources and financing to women casting out on their own. Other good starting points for women and minorities: American Woman's Economic Development Corporation (800-222-2933); National Association for Female Executives (212-477-2200) and the U.S. Department of Commerce's Minority Business Development Agency (202-482-1936).

363 FREE (OR ALMOST FREE) INFORMATION ON FRANCHISING.

If you are considering buying a franchise, you can get a free copy of the company's Uniform Franchise Offering Circular. It will contain a list of current franchisees. You may want to contact some organizations that lobby for franchisee rights:
The American Franchisee Association 800-334-4AFA;
American Association of Franchisees and Dealers 800-733-9858.

A company that sells reports on franchises is Frandata (1155 Connecticut Ave. N.W., Suite 275, Washington, D.C. 20036; 202-659-8640 or fax 202-457-0618).

364 FREE INFO ON STARTING A HOME-BASED BUSINESS.

If you are considering a startup from home, you can get some terrific help at no-cost – even from the IRS. Pick up its New Business Tax Kit at a local IRS office or call 800-829-1040 for more information.

The Small Business Administration (800-827-5722) has a wealth of information, including booklets on business plans, a directory of state small business programs, and planning and goal setting for small businesses. To order, write for free forms 115A and 115B at the Small Business Administration, 409 Third St. S.W., Washington, D.C. 20416.

To avoid pesky work-at-home scams, write: The Council of Better Business Bureaus, Inc., 4200 Wilson Blvd., Suite 800, Arlington, Va. 22203; 703-276-0100. Send $2 plus a SASE and request Tips on Work-at-Home Schemes.

365 IF YOU OWN A SMALL BUSINESSS, CONSIDER WORKING AT HOME.

No longer do most clients think it odd for entrepreneurs to work from home. You can have a great office essentially for free, plus get tax breaks. Several organizations offer valuable advice and support:

American Association of Home Based Businesses, P.O. Box 10023, Rockville, Md. 20849-0023 or 800-447-9710.

The National Association for Cottage Industry (312-472-8116 or send a SASE to: P.O. Box 14850, Chicago, Ill. 60614) has a newsletter, group health insurance, advice on homeowners insurance with special coverage for home-based businesses.

The National Federation of Independent Business (202-554-9000 or Suite 700, 600 Maryland Ave. S.W., Washington, D.C. 20024; dues start at $100 a year) is a lobbying group for 600,000 small business owners. Members receive a free bimonthly magazine and frequent updates on legislation affecting small business.

366 BARGAINS FROM BUSINESSES THAT WENT BUST.

What many would-be entrepreneurs don't know is that you can get great deals of business equipment from an unexpected source: the Small Business Administration (800-827-5722). If that agency has made a loan to a business that goes into foreclosure, it gets some of the goodies left over from the bankruptcy proceedings. Contact your local SBA office for more information about SBA auctions.

367 FREE INFORMATION ON THE AMERICANS WITH DISABILITIES ACT.

To get a free package of ADA compliance information, plus a pamphlet called Employer Incentives, which has tax and hiring credit information, contact the President's Committee on Employment of People with Disabilities (1331 F St. N.W., #300, Washington, D.C. 20004; 202-376-6200). The committee's Job Accommodation Network (800-526-7234) offers free, confidential advice from consultants to businesses on how to best utilize disabled workers. Consultants will explain assisted devices, modifying work stations, job sharing and more. You can also get a free information pack from the hotline.

368 HOW TO FIND DEALS ON OFFICE AND HEAVY EQUIPMENT.

Need a used tractor fast? For a line on a variety of used equipment, try Heartland Communications ($29.95 for a one-year subscription; 800-247-2000), which publishes eight different buy/sell weekly publications geared to industries including contracting, heavy construction and aviation. Penton Publications publishes the Used Equipment Directory (one-year subscription with 12 issues: $45 for first class; $30 for third class; 800-526-6052), which lists availability from dealers nationwide. A good buy is The Office Equipment Adviser

($19.95 plus $3 shipping) updated annually in August and published by What to Buy for Business, Inc. (P.O. Box 22857, Santa Barbara, Calif. 93105; 800-247-2185). This 600-page book covers every imaginable item you'd need for your office. Or, if you are interested in a specific product like phones or low-volume copiers, call and ask about its single topic publications, which include model-specific information and productivity testing results. These magazines are $23 each.

For office furniture at a discount, look in the Yellow Pages for companies that remanufacture office furniture.

Top office furniture manufacturers also sell remanufactured furniture. Call Phoenix Designs, at 800-253-2733, which remanufactures popular Herman Miller desks and chairs or contact Remark at 616-538-8120. Revest (404-352-0476) remanufactures and sells the well-known Steelcase furniture.

Another terrific source to get suppliers of new and used materials and equipment is through a clearinghouse called Pacific Materials Exchange Network at 509-466-1019.

369 BILL PHONE CALLS TO CLIENTS PROPERLY.

If you work from home, divvying up your phone bill can be a chore. Find out about free call accounting service from your phone company. It'll require you to punch in a few extra numbers before each call but will save you time in the long run.

370 FREE INFORMATION ON KEEPING YOUR EMPLOYEES SAFE AND IMPROVING THEIR HEALTH.

Contact the National Safety Council for free booklets and brochures on safety issues. Call 708-775-2307 or write the Public Relations Dept., 1121 Spring Lake Drive, Itasca, Ill. 60143. The council will provide free consulting, videos and newsletters geared to your industry as well.

371 GET FINANCING FOR YOUR BUSINESS.

Looking for an investor in your business? The Investment Division of the U.S. Small Business Administration publishes a free Directory of Small Business Investment Companies, which lists names, addresses, telephone numbers and investment policies of these angels. Write: Investment Division, U.S. Small Business Administration, 409 Third St. S.W., Suite 6300, Washington, D.C. 20416; 202-205-6510.

Here is a sampling of angels:

The Capital Network, Inc. 512-794-9398

Investors' Circle 708-876-1101 (deals only with socially responsible startups)

Pacific Venture Capital 714-509-2990

Seed Capital Network Inc. 615-573-4655

Technology Capital Network at MIT 617-253-7163

VentureLine 518-486-5438.

If you're on the hunt for cash to launch your dream business, try the Small Business Source Book ($260, Gale Research, 800-877-4253), which lists state and federal government programs; Gibbs Publishing ($19.95, 707-448-0270; Box 1120, Vacaville, Calif. 95696) does a directory of federal loans and grants for small businesses; the American Bankers Association (800-338-06260 publishes SBA Lending Made Easy; $59 for members; non-members, $89); Pratt's Guide to Venture Capital Sources ($225, Venture Economics, 212-765-5311) and the Directory of Incentives for Business Investment and Development in the United States: A State by State Guide ($145, National Association of State Development Agencies, 202-898-1302).

Other good contacts:

National Association of Small Business Investment Companies (1199 N. Fairfax St., Suite 200, Alexandria, Va. 22314; 703-683-1601 or fax 703-683-1605) publishes Venture Capital:

Where to Find It (to order send a $10 check or money order to NASBIC Directory, P.O. Box 2039, Merrifield, Va. 22116). The book lists more than 160 SBICs.

AI Research Corporation (415-852-9140) has a database with 1,300 U.S. sources of venture capital ($89.95; IBM compatible).

National Venture Capital Association (703-351-5269).

372 GET A FREE PIECE OF EXPERIENCED MINDS.

Computer networks are great places to get free advice from professionals. Four times a week, Michael Seid, a franchise consultant who bills clients $250-300 an hour, logs onto CompuServe (800-848-8990 or 800-848-8199; first month free, regularly $9.95 a month) and answers queries about franchising. CompuServe has more than 600 forums on-line.

Another source: America Online (800-827-6364: 10 hours free, which is a $40 value plus free startup software). To order America Online, call 800-225-5461 or fax 800-827-4595 or write America Online, 8619 Westwood Center Drive, Vienna, Calif. 22182-9806.

Another good way to tap into free advice from experts is to look up the specialty in The Encyclopedia of Associations (Gale Research), available at your local library.

373 SOFTWARE FOR FREE.

Who says you have to shell out major bucks for software? Hundreds of shareware programs are available on Internet and other on-line services, through local computer user groups and mail order. Basically, here's how it works. You obtain the software for nada, try it out, then if you like it, send a small registration fee (usually under $100) to the software copyright owner. If you want a good overview, send $7.50 for postage for a catalog on disk with more than 1,200 shareware programs from the Association of Shareware Professionals, 545 Grover Road, Muskegon, Mich. 49442-9427; 616-788-5131/fax 616-788-2765/CompuServe 72050,1433. Or for $26.95 you can request a computer disk loaded with 1,200 programs. Or check out Glossbrenner's Guide to Shareware for Small Businesses (800-822-8158; $37.95 plus tax and handling, McGraw-Hill Ordering Services, 860 Taylor Station Road, Blacklick, Ohio 43004).

You can also request a free shareware catalog from Reasonable Solutions (800-876-3475). Before you buy software, call the manufacturer's toll-free numbers and request a free "working model." This version is streamlined and allows you to test out the software before making a serious investment.

The New England Business Service (800-225-9540) puts out a free Directory of Software with almost 1,000 listings. Another option: Fill in all survey cards related to your computer purchases. Software manufacturers tag certain users as important and will begin to send you products to test for them. After buying a Macintosh recently, a customer got an offer in the mail from a small company called Ohio Distinctive Software (614-459-0453) to pay $8 for three programs retailing for $218.95. The company even offered a money-back guarantee.

Microsoft particularly likes to test products with computer consultants in the hope that the consultants will then tout the products to their clients. One consultant with whom we spoke is part of a formalized program with Microsoft (800-426-9400) called the Beta program. Another consultant regularly communicates with small software makers, explaining his business. In return, he has gotten everything from accounting to writing business plan software—all for the price of a toll-free phone call, in other words, zip. He simply looked for ads in professional magazines and called companies: "They'll even send you upgrades to keep you in the loop," he says delightedly.

374 TAKE ADVANTAGE OF OTHERS' LIQUID ASSETS.

For information on government auctions, here are some sources: Contact your local office of the SBA and ask for the liquidation officer. Ask the local IRS office for the 24-hour Auction Hotline number. Write to the Defense Department at BRMS, Dept. of Defense, National Sales Office, P.O. Box 5275—DDRC, 2163 Airways Blvd., Memphis, Tenn. 38114-5210.

375 EXPERT ADVICE FOR CORPORATE GIFT GIVING

Stumped over what to get for that special client? Many companies have added professional gift consultants to their staffs. Try *Tiffany & Co.* (800-423-2394) or *Hammacher Schlemmer* (312-649-7334). Other experts who will give you free advice include: *Alliance Gift Consultants* (800-443-8688); *The Corporate Presence of New York* (212-989-6446); *Prize Possessions* (800-283-1166) and *Wishes Under Wraps* (212-628-4962).

376 MAIL-ORDER SOFTWARE.

You can save substantially on software by purchasing it through the mail. Here are some top companies:
Telemart, 8804 N. 23rd Ave., Phoenix, Ariz. 85021; 800-426-6659;
PC Connection 800-243-8088;
Mac Connection, 6 Mill St., Marlow, N.H. 03456; 800-MAC-LISA.

377 FREE LEGAL ADVICE FOR HOME-BASED BUSINESS OWNERS.

Write for Legal Barriers to Home-Based Work, available from the National Center for Policy Analysis, 7701 N. Stemmons, Suite 800, Dallas, Texas 75247. Also, ask the SBA for a free copy of Selecting the Legal Structure for Your Business.

378 SWITCHING FROM DOS TO MICROSOFT.

If the dominant computer company in the world sounds better to you, but you are still stuck in the world of DOS, you can find out more about how your business would change with Microsoft by calling 800-60-SOURCE. Experts will discuss your business needs with you and then send you either a free copy of Planning the Move or Making the Move kit.

379 CLUBS FOR HOME OFFICE DWELLERS.

The AT&T Home Business Resources (800-383-6164) offers several perks, including Powersource magazine. Egghead Software (800-344-4323) has a free discount club that entitles you to a free catalog with special discounts each month.

380 INDUSTRIAL WORK CLOTHES FOR LESS.

Clothes designed for work are often longer lasting and make great casual wear. Check out Wear Guard (for a free catalog call 800-388-3300). This company has a large selection of jackets, belts, shoes, flannel shirt-jackets, aprons, boots, thermal underwear and much more. Plus, it does monograms and logos. Discounts are as much as 30% off and it gives a valuable free gift with a minimum order of $35.

381 GET OFFICE SUPPLIES AT HALF PRICE.

You can get great deals on everything from staples to fax machines at places like Staples and Office Depot. Or try some of the mail-order companies like:
Viking Office Products, 5101 Statesman Drive, Irving, Texas 75063 or 800-421-1222 or fax 800-762-7329 (free delivery);
Wholesale Supply Company 800-962-9162.

Here are some good companies for bargains on office supplies:
Office Depot 800-800-5243 (The company also has a special long distance deal available for small businesses.)

Office Max 800-788-8080

Quill 800-789-1331 (This company also produces free booklets on topics of interest to business people.)

382 THE NATION'S BIGGEST JOB LISTING.

The federal government hires more than 10,000 new employees a month, but these jobs are unadvertised. The only way to find out about them is a subscription to the Federal Jobs Digest ($34 for three months, tax deductible; satisfaction or your money back). Call toll-free at 800-824-5000 for your copy.

383 FREE INSURANCE ADVICE.

If you are self-employed, you may be able to get lower insurance rates by joining a group like one of the following:

National Association for the Self-Employed, 2121 Precinct Line Road, Hurst, Texas 76054 or 800-827-9990;

National Organization of Women 202-331-0066;

Small Business Service Bureau 800-343-0939.

To get a free list of publications on insurance, send a SASE to the Consumer Federation of America Insurance Group, 414 A St. S.E., Washington, D.C. 20003 or call 202-547-6426 or fax 202-547-5427. The Health Insurance Association of America (202-824-1600; 555 13th St. N.W., Suite 600 East, Washington, D.C. 20004) also offers numerous helpful booklets.

If you are into holistic medicine, try the Alternative Health Insurance Services at 818-702-0888, which locates insurers willing to reimburse for alternative providers like chiropractors.

384 SKIP COSTLY AND TIME-CONSUMING TRIPS TO THE POST OFFICE.

You can buy stamps by calling 800-STAMPS24 and charging them to your MasterCard or Visa, thereby also giving yourself a convenient record of the purchase so you can deduct it from your taxes (if you are self-employed).

385 FREE CONTACTS.

One of the nicest things you can do for yourself is to make new connections with people. Look in the career opportunity section of your local newspaper, and you'll find a calendar of free networking opportunities. Great jobs, nifty assignments and new friends are what you'll get in return for investing some of your time. Here are some national networking organizations:

Leads Club, P.O. Box 24, Carlsbad, Calif. 92008; 619-434-3761; $75 initiation fee; $21 a month dues;

National Assocation of Women Business Owners, 175 West Jackson Blvd., Suite 625, Chicago, Ill. 60604; 312-322-0990;

The Network, 2685 S. Bucknell Ave., Clairmont, Calif. 91711; 800-825-8286.

386 LOW-COST REPORTS ON FRANCHISING.

If you are interested in franchising, which now accounts for almost half of all retail sales in this nation, getting unbiased information can be extremely difficult. Request what is called a disclosure document from the franchisor. Then you may want to consider getting a "Just the Facts" report for $69 each from Marketdata Enterprises, Inc. (181 S. Franklin Ave., Suite 608, Valley Stream, N.Y. 11580; 516-791-6559 or fax 516-791-7759.) You can charge it to your credit card. The company offers 12 reports on businesses ranging from day care to real estate.

387 GET DEEP DISCOUNTS ON MAGAZINES.

If you are an information junkie, call your favorite magazines' toll-free numbers and ask if they offer a professional rate for small business owners. For instance, Newsweek offers such a break, giving subscribers a year's subscription for $38, more than $100 off its regular rate.

If staying in the information loop is important to your business, but you don't like going to the library to do your reading, consider making a trip to your local recycling center, like Marc Eisenson and Nancy Castleman, who write The Pocket Change Investor (914-758-1400 or 800-255-0899), a newsletter on living frugally. Each month the couple scoops up several dozen publications, free of charge. You can also try asking your hairdresser or doctor to give you magazines at the end of the month.

388 SHAVE YOUR PHONE BILLS BY SMART CALLING.

If the phone is a critical link in your business, consider changing your office hours slightly and making calls or faxing to the opposite coast to take advantage of the long distance breaks you get if you call before 9 a.m. or after 5 p.m. One children's clothing designer returns calls to the West Coast after she puts her daughters to bed at 8 p.m. eastern standard time, thus saving a mint on her phone bill. Also, skip the full-size, cutesy fax cover sheets. They waste valuable transmission time and money.

389 GET TAX BREAKS FOR DONATIONS.

Don't let excess inventory or outdated equipment gather dust when they could reap you other benefits—namely tax deductions. Contact the National Association for the Exchange of Industrial Resources at 800-562-0955 to find out about worthy causes that could take your donations and give you the necessary tax documentation to prove your generosity.

390 HELP YOURSELF BY HELPING YOUR EMPLOYEES.

You may not be able to afford an employee assistance program that large companies often have, but you can still provide help to your workers, cutting absenteeism and boosting productivity in the process. Ask for a free kit called "Making Your

Workplace Drug Free" from the U.S. Public Health Service's Center for Substance Abuse Prevention (800-843-4971).

One restaurant owner looked up several free hotlines and other help providers and keeps the numbers in his desk, so that he can easily refer employees to these resources.

391 FREE ADVICE ON DOING BUSINESS ON THE INTERNET.

You can get a free paper called "How to Do Business on the Internet" by calling 800-558-7656 Dept. B1. You can also request a copy of the Internet $9 Cruise, which lets you sign up for the Internet and gets you a dozen easy-to-use Windows applications including WebSurfer.

392 A FREE GUIDE TO STREAMLINING YOUR ACCOUNTING PROCESSES.

You can get an 80-page guide on tracking cash flow, reducing repetitive data entry and other accounting issues by contacting RealWorld Accounting and Business Software (800-678-6336).

393 FREE SHIPPING SOFTWARE.

Even if your business is relatively tiny, you can get a free copy of FedEx Ship software for Windows or Macintosh. It will track and confirm package deliveries, print labels on your own laser printer and maintain a database of your customers. Call 800-GO-FEDEX.

394 FIND OUT IF ELECTRONIC MAIL COULD SAVE YOU MONEY.

If you haven't converted to the technology revolution, request free copies of The Electronic Mail Advantage: Applications and Benefits, three booklets, each about 30 pages, from the

Electronic Messaging Association, 1655 N. Fort Myer Drive, Suite 850, Arlington, Va. 22209; 703-524-5550.

395 GET EXPERT ADVICE ON WAYS TO SAVE WHEN YOU START YOUR BUSINESS.

An excellent newsletter that has dozens of handy tips on making startups fly with as little capital as possible is called Bootstrappin' Entrepreneur (Research Done Write!, Suite B261-EM, 8726 South Sepulveda Blvd., Los Angeles, Calif. 90045-4082 or 310-568-9861; $30 a year for the quarterly; a sample issue is $8). Written and published by Kimberly Stansell, the newsletter highlights free products and services, business-building tips and more for small businesses. Recent tips: You can get free samples of Post-it Tape Flags and Post-it Fax Notes from 3M by faxing your name, business name, address and phone number to 612-633-7092.

396 FREE HELP ON EXPORTING.

Small businesses sometimes assume doing business overseas is out of reach. Contact the Export Opportunity Hotline (800-243-7232) to reach a specialist who can give you free guidance on many aspects of exporting and can make referrals.

397 FREE WORKERS FOR YOUR BUSINESS.

Give high school and college kids an employment opportunity by offering internships at your business. You'll have to fulfill some educational requirements, but you'll get temporary help for no or low cost depending on the opportunities you provide. The National Society of Experiential Education (3509 Haworth Drive, Suite 207, Raleigh, N.C. 27609; 919-787-3263) provides free information about setting up such a program.

398 FREE GUIDE TO RESOURCES FOR SMALL COMPANIES.

Tip from the Bootstrappin' Entrepreneur: You can get a free book from IBM that lists hundreds of useful resources—both government and private sector—for small businesses. Write IBM Corporation, C. Piebes, Mail Drop 325—Resource Guide, 1133 Westchester Ave., White Plains, N.Y. 10604.

399 FREE MAGAZINE FROM THE SMALL BUSINESS ADMINISTRATION.

This, too, from Bootstrappin' Enterpreneur: Once a year Pacific Bell teams up with the SBA to produce a magazine called Small Business Success. The 81-page magazine with helpful topics like "The Ancient Art of Bartering Goes Mainstream" and a resource directory is free if you call 800-848-8000 (press option 2).

400 FREE BOOK FOR HOME OFFICE DWELLERS.

When you subscribe to Home Office Computing, you get a terrific book, The Home Office Answer Guide, free. Call 800-288-7812 (one year is $16.97).

INDEX

Order Form
400 Steals Beyond Belief
by Eric W. Gershman

(please print)

Date _____

Name _____

Address _____

City _____ State _____ Zip _____

Phone (_____) _____

400 Steals Beyond Belief
Eric W. Gershman

Price	Quantity	Amount
$12.00		
	Subtotal	
For delivery in Massachusetts Add $.60 cents sales tax per book		
Shipping & Handling 1st Book $2.00 Add'l Books $1.00 *Note: Free freight when ordering two or more cartons*		
TOTAL		

Payment Method

_____ Check or money order enclosed. Please make payable to:

Financial Answers Network, Inc.

Please return this form to:

Financial Answers, Inc.
129 South Street
Suite 300
Boston, MA
Or call 1-800-411-6789 to place your order.